STATE V. BAKER

Third Edition

STATE V. BAKER

Third Edition

Joseph E. Taylor

University of the Pacific
McGeorge School of Law

NATIONAL INSTITUTE FOR TRIAL ADVOCACY

Address inquiries to:
Reprint Permission
National Institute for Trial Advocacy
1685 38th Street, Suite 200
Boulder, CO 80301-2735
Phone: (800) 225-6482
Fax: (720) 890-7069
E-mail: permissions@nita.org

ISBN 978-1-60156-294-4
FBA 1294

CONTENTS

ACKNOWLEDGMENTS

The author would like to acknowledge the special contribution to the development of this case made by Robert Anthony, MD, and Mark Fajardo, MD, of the Northern California Forensic Pathology Medical Corporation, both recognized experts in forensic pathology. They supplied specialized information that was especially helpful in preparing both the prosecution and defense expert reports and greatly assisted the author in formulating the case.

Bruce Moran, a criminalist with the Sacramento County District Attorney's Crime Laboratory, provided expert advice on the issues covered in the forensic scientific report and expert testimony of the witness Dale Ryan.

Chris Hadley, assistant manager of the Property Section of the Sacramento Police Department, provided information and assistance in preparing the weapon evidence in this case.

Cynthia Re, a former student at McGeorge School of Law and practicing attorney, assisted greatly in preparing and compiling case materials and offering invaluable suggestions.

The graphics including the cover, the diagram, and maps were all prepared by Lori Hall, head of the Graphics Department of McGeorge School of Law.

Thanks also to the 1947 Boston Braves for providing the last names of all characters in the *State v. Baker* case.

INTRODUCTION

This is a criminal case in which Sarah Baker, the daughter of a billionaire international arms dealer, has been charged with the first-degree murder of her husband, Kelly Baker, a well-known Nita City television news anchor at station KNTA-TV, in violation of § 101 of the Criminal Code of the State of Nita. On September 7, 2012, Sarah Baker shot her husband Kelly Baker in the kitchen of their large estate known as Ashgate Farm near Warrenton, Nita. Kelly Baker was found lying facedown on the floor. A nine-mm Luger pistol was found on the floor near Kelly Baker's body, and a butcher knife was in Kelly Baker's right hand. Four bullet wounds were found in the chest and neck area.

In her statement to the sheriff's investigator, Sarah Baker said her husband had accused her of having a romantic relationship with Bradley McCormick, the chief deputy district attorney of Darrow County. She denied the relationship, explaining that she had worked with McCormick to establish a new center for battered women through the organization she chaired. She said that on the morning of September 7 she was in the kitchen just after 8:00 a.m. when her husband entered the kitchen and brandished a semi-automatic pistol and said that he was going to kill her for being unfaithful. She was able to convince him to put the gun on the table. Sarah Baker then said that she grabbed the gun to protect herself, and as soon as she did, Kelly Baker then grabbed a kitchen knife, screamed obscenities, and advanced toward her, threatening to kill her. She said he slashed her left arm with the knife. As he came after her, she fired to protect herself, shooting him four times. A defense forensic pathologist has concluded that the autopsy findings are completely consistent with Sarah Baker's version of the facts.

The State contends that Sarah Baker intended to divorce Kelly Baker and to cut him out of her will, and Kelly Baker told her he would bring legal action to seek a large portion of her estate. For that reason, the State claims, Sarah Baker decided to kill Kelly Baker and then attempted to cover up her crime by slashing her own left arm and planting a knife in Kelly Baker's hand. An autopsy examination showed that Kelly Baker suffered fatal wounds to the neck and chest as well as wounds to his right arm and back. Three shots hit him at downward angles. The State's forensic pathologist concluded that the gunshots were consistent with Kelly Baker being seated when he was shot and further concluded that the three to four knife wounds on Sarah Baker's left arm were superficial and were consistent with wounds that had been self-inflicted. A State's firearm examiner concluded that the absence of gunpowder residue on Kelly Baker's clothing meant that Sarah Baker was more than four feet from Kelly Baker when she fired.

The applicable law is contained in the proposed jury instructions set forth at the end of the file.

Special Instructions for Use as a Full Trial

When this case file is used for a full trial, each party is limited to calling the following witnesses:

State of Nita:
Kit Manville
Detective Lee Holmes
Dr. Morgan Sain
Forensic Scientist Dale Ryan

Defendant:
Sarah Baker
Dr. Leslie Torgeson
Bradley McCormick
Chris Spahn

Discovery Obligations

Pursuant to Nita C.C. § 1054.3, which requires the defense to disclose names, addresses, relevant written statements, and reports of witnesses the defense intends to call at trial, the reports of defense witnesses Bradley McCormick, Chris Spahn, and Dr. Torgeson have been disclosed to the prosecution.

Pursuant to Nita C.C. § 1054.2, Nita Police Department case reports were disclosed to the defense by the prosecution.

Required Stipulations

1. The defendant Sarah Baker is female. Bradley McCormick is male. All other witnesses may be either male or female.

2. The Search Warrant Inventory and Return are true, accurate, and complete copies of the originals filed with the court by Detective Holmes and meet the requirements of Federal Rules of Evidence 1002 and 1003.

3. The transcript of the 911 call is an accurate and complete transcript of the call made by the defendant to the Sheriff's Department at 8:51 a.m. on September 7, 2012.

4. The "Last Will and Testament" is a true, accurate, and complete copy of the only will prepared by the defendant.

5. The report of Senior Identification Technician Robin Mulligan is admissible as evidence. Counsel will stipulate to the qualifications of Mulligan to render the opinions set forth in Mulligan's report.

PRETRIAL MOTIONS

The defendant moved to suppress all statements she made to Detective Holmes on Fifth, Sixth, and Fourteenth Amendment grounds. The court ruled that the statement given at 1010 hours was admissible, but the defendant's comments at 1700 hours exercising her right not to talk were inadmissible. The court also denied defendant's motion to suppress evidence seized pursuant to the search warrant as well as any present in-court testimony based on such evidence as the product of a violation of the Fourth and Fourteenth Amendments. These legal issues may not be relitigated at trial.

IN THE DISTRICT COURT
OF THE STATE OF NITA
COUNTY OF DARROW

THE STATE OF NITA	)	
	)	Case No. CR 2201-05
vs.	)	
	)	INFORMATION
SARAH H. BAKER,	)	
Defendant.	)	
	)	

THE STATE OF NITA does hereby charge the defendant, SARAH HANNA BAKER, with the following offense under the Criminal Code of the State of Nita:

That on 7th day of September, 2012, at and within the County of Darrow and within the boundaries of Nita City, SARAH HANNA BAKER committed the crime of Murder in the First Degree, a felony, in violation of Section 101 of the Criminal Code of the State of Nita, in that she did knowingly, willfully, feloniously, and deliberately and with the intent to cause the death of Kelly Baker, caused the death of Kelly Baker, a human being, contrary to the form, force, and effect of the law of the State of Nita and against the peace and dignity of the People of the State of Nita.

DATED: October 25, 2012

Elton Voiselle

Ella Marie Wright, Attorney General
By Elton Voiselle, Deputy Attorney General
State of Nita

Exhibit 1

TRANSCRIPT OF 911 CALL FROM SARAH BAKER SEPTEMBER 7, 2012, AT 8:51 A.M.

The following is a verbatim transcript of the call received by Dispatcher Karl of the Darrow County Sheriff's Department from Sarah Baker at 8:51 a.m. on September 7, 2012:

Karl: 911, where's your emergency?

Baker: Ah, yes. I need . . . I need to report a . . . a shot man and he's dead.

Karl: Where at?

Baker: He's at Ashgate Farm and. . . .

Karl: What's the address?

Baker: 8714 Springs Road. Ashgate Farm.

Karl: OK, what's his name?

Baker: Ah . . . Kelly Baker. He's my husband.

Karl: OK, did you just find him or. . . .

Baker: He tried to kill me.

Karl: OK, did you shoot him?

Baker: I . . . I had a gun, yes.

Karl: Did you shoot him?

Baker: I think he's dead.

Karl: OK. Is anybody else in the house with you or anything?

Baker: Nobody at this time.

Karl: Can you tell me ah . . . have you had problems before?

Baker: Yes, I have.

Karl: OK. Where's the, ah, weapon at, ma'am?

Baker: It's . . . it's on the floor in the kitchen.

Karl: OK. I just want to make sure you don't have it when the deputy shows up' cause you might be a little antsy when the deputy gets there, so you just want to make sure that you don't have it.

Baker: No, it's . . . it's on . . . it's on the floor.

Baker: Chris . . . Chris, please come here. Don't go in the kitchen. Kelly is dead. . . .

Karl: Right. . . .

Baker: . . . I'm on the phone. Please, Chris. . . .

Karl: Right, make sure nobody goes into the kitchen.

Baker: The sheriffs are coming right away, Chris. Sit down. Sit down.

Karl: Make sure nobody goes in there.

Baker: No. Nobody, nobody . . . .

Karl: OK, ma'am, I need you to come out the front door . . . .

Baker: OK.

Karl: . . . and meet with the deputy.

Baker: OK, I will.

Karl: OK.

Baker: I . . . I'll hang up now.

Karl: OK, that's fine.

EXHIBIT 2 – THE KNIFE FOUND IN KELLY BAKER'S RIGHT HAND

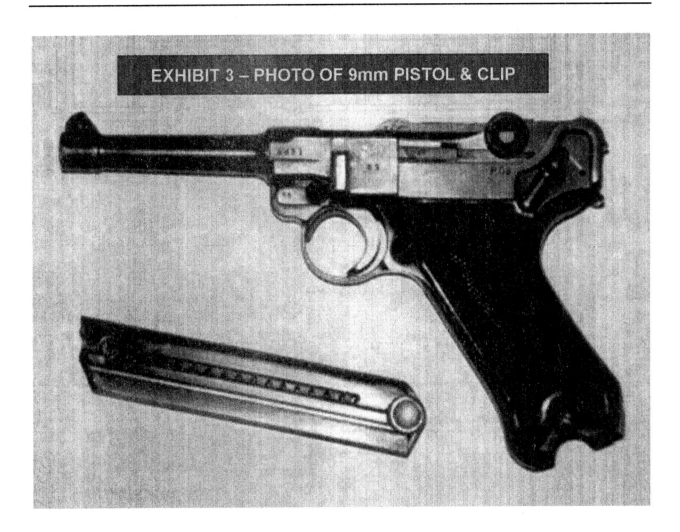

EXHIBIT 3 – PHOTO OF 9mm PISTOL & CLIP

EXHIBIT 4 – ASHGATE FARM MAIN HOUSE

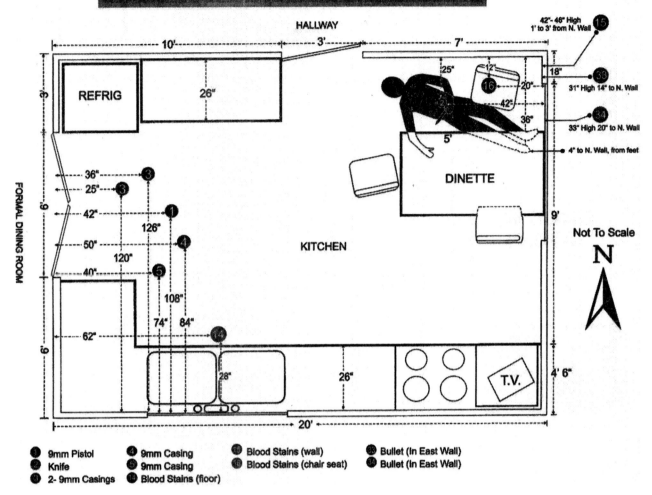

EXHIBIT 5 – DIAGRAM OF KITCHEN AT ASHGATE

1 9mm Pistol
2 Knife
3 2- 9mm Casings
4 9mm Casing
5 9mm Casing
14 Blood Stains (floor)
15 Blood Stains (wall)
16 Blood Stains (chair seat)
33 Bullet (In East Wall)
34 Bullet (In East Wall)

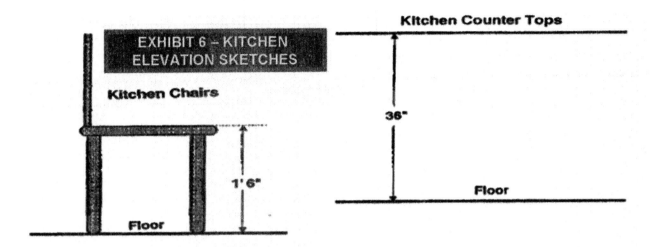

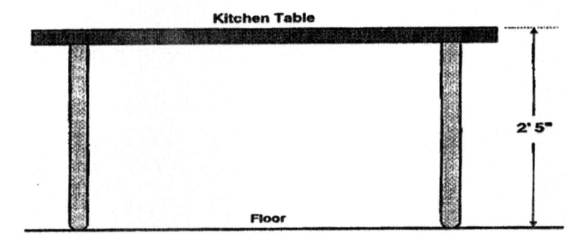

EXHIBIT 7 – DIAGRAM OF ASHGATE HOME

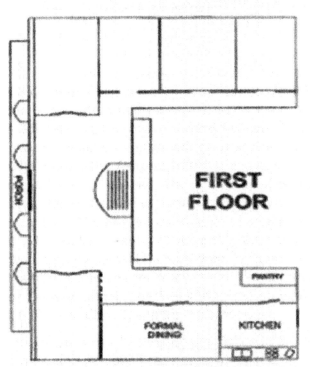

DIAGRAM OF ASHGATE HOM

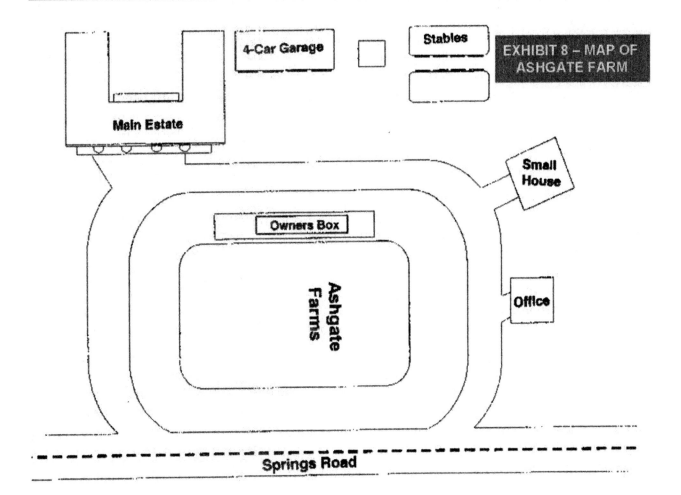

DARROW COUNTY SHERIFF'S DEPARTMENT
OFFENSE REPORT

FILE NUMBER:	05–28088
VICTIM:	Kelly Lawrence Baker 8714 Springs Road Warrenton, Nita
SUSPECT:	Sarah Hanna Baker
LOCATION:	Ashgate Farm 8714 Springs Road Warrenton, Nita
OFFENSE:	CC 187—Murder
DATE OF REPORT:	September 7, 2012
BY:	Detective Lee Holmes Badge Number 114 *LH*

DETAILS OF OFFENSE

Facts

At 0852 hours I was at the Darrow County Sheriff's Detective Division preparing an investigative report in an attempted rape case when I received a radio call from Dispatcher Karl to respond immediately to a homicide scene at Ashgate Farm near Warrenton. I communicated via radio with Deputy Camelli, who informed me that she was enroute and would control the scene. I arrived at 0910 hours. The Ashgate estate is approximately 350 acres and includes a very large two-story home, which is U-shaped, and a number of outbuildings, including a four-car garage and several stables. Deputy Camelli was standing with a woman I learned was Sarah Baker and with Chris Spahn. Deputy Camelli informed me that she had met Sarah Baker and Chris Spahn upon arrival at 0857 hours. Ms. Baker was standing outside the home at the front entrance door when Deputy Camelli arrived. Deputy Camelli then entered the home and was unable to locate any other people present in the house. She saw the body of Kelly Baker, Ms. Baker's husband, lying facedown on the kitchen floor. Deputy Camelli checked and found no vital signs. Deputy Camelli then waited outside with Ms. Baker and Chris Spahn for my arrival.

I then entered the kitchen of the Baker home and saw a nine-mm Luger semiautomatic pistol and four nine-mm shell casings in front of the refrigerator and two bullet holes in the wall near Mr. Baker's body, which was lying facedown in a pool of blood. I also noticed what appeared to be a kitchen knife in Mr. Baker's right hand, which was under his body. I took possession of the casings;

the pistol, serial number 6851, which had three live rounds in the magazine and one in the chamber; and the knife and placed them in an evidence bag.

I saw that Ms. Baker had scratches and bright red blood on her left arm. Ms. Baker requested permission to change her shoes in an upstairs bedroom. I accompanied her and placed her bloodstained, white canvas sneakers in an evidence bag. I then communicated with Dispatcher Karl, who informed me of the contents of the 911 call Karl had received from Ms. Baker. Deputy Coroner Clem Beazley and County Forensic Pathologist Dr. Sain arrived, entered the kitchen, and took custody of the body of Kelly Baker, the deceased husband of Sarah Baker. The Coroner's Office personnel left. Based on my examination of the scene and my understanding of the 911 conversation between Dispatcher Karl and Ms. Baker, I arrested Ms. Baker for murder and transported her to the Darrow County Jail, where she was booked and printed. At the County Jail and in my presence, Ms. Baker was observed by County Nurse Alex Nelson. Ms. Baker's left arm was washed, and the nurse confirmed that the cuts were not life threatening and did not require sutures or bandaging. Nurse Nelson took samples of hair and a blood sample from Ms. Baker. Nurse Nelson removed Ms. Baker's clothing from the dressing room and handed it to me for safekeeping as evidence. I took custody of one pair of women's slacks and a short-sleeved blouse. Ms. Baker was issued a pair of standard jail overalls.

Statement of Sarah Baker

At 1010 hours I fully informed Ms. Baker of her rights under the *Miranda* decision. Ms. Baker told me that she understood those rights and was willing to tell me what happened. She said that the events this morning were the culmination of several weeks of disagreements she and her husband had. She said that it was important that I understand the background of their marriage. In 2008 she met Kelly. At the time she was a successful producer of polo ponies, and she was an avid polo fan. At her Ashgate estate every July she held an annual charity polo event known as the "Community Games." The funds were to be distributed to local charities. Kelly Baker was covering the event for KNTA, and he interviewed her. The two began to see each other more, and one year later they were married. The two lived at her estate, and Kelly drove to Nita City from Warrenton every workday. Because of Kelly's schedule, they began to see less and less of each other.

In August 2011 she felt it was necessary that she become more occupied, and she accepted an offer to become the unpaid director of Project WEB, a nonprofit organization devoted to protecting battered women. She realized that she was in a position, because of her wealth and her influence, to develop more funding for the organization. In early 2012 the board of directors authorized her to develop a new center or home for battered women. She began meeting with community leaders to coordinate the plan. During this process she met Bradley McCormick, the chief deputy district attorney of Darrow County. McCormick introduced her to others in the county government, and a Darrow County Battered Women Council was formed. Ms. Baker and McCormick co-chaired the council, and as a consequence they met on a regular basis to plan or implement the effort. Ms. Baker said that while she greatly admires McCormick, she had no romantic feelings for him, and she was sure that he had none for her.

In July 2011 she was also once again hosting the Community Games at her estate. However, this year a good deal of the charity income was earmarked for the WEB Center. Bradley McCormick attended and sat in the owner's box with her. Kelly was not present, as he had other work. After the event, Ms. Baker and McCormick conferred about the proceeds, and they had a "working dinner" at a nearby restaurant. There were others at the restaurant who knew Kelly, and apparently someone mentioned this to Kelly. He became especially irate and called her a lot of bad names. She was surprised, because she had never seen this side of Kelly before, but he became very ugly and abusive. Kelly said that he didn't believe her lies and said that she was his wife, and if he found out that she was cheating, she would need to spend some time in this fancy new center she was building. The uglier Kelly became, the more damage this did to their relationship. For the last several weeks she tried to avoid him, and the only contact she had with him was when she would occasionally see him for breakfast or for dinner. The cook prepared the meals, and because they had separate bedrooms, they did not have that much direct contact.

About one week ago Kelly called her from work and told her he expected her to be there when he got home. He arrived about 11:00 p.m., and he had been drinking. He said that she was making a fool of him, and he had heard that she had been "fooling around with McCormick" at their home. She told Kelly that McCormick had been there several times for planning sessions for the center and again told him that he was imagining things, that there was nothing romantic between them. Kelly reached over and picked up a china lamp that was a family heirloom and said, "This is what I think of your lies," and threw the lamp against the fireplace. She cried and ran from the house, got in her car, and drove to the home of Chris Spahn, the manager of Ashgate Farm, where she stayed the night.

Ms. Baker said she began to realize that she had no real marriage, and she began to fear that Kelly would hurt or kill her. She thought about the fact that she had a will prepared shortly after her marriage leaving virtually her entire estate to Kelly. She decided to contact her lawyer and revise the will to cut Kelly out of the will except for a summer house and a car. She said nothing for several days, and on September 6, Kelly called her from work and told her to be home when he got there. They met in the early evening. Ms. Baker and Chris Spahn were finishing a discussion on the front porch when Kelly arrived. He had been drinking, and without waiting for Chris to leave, he snarled, "So you're going to cut me out of the will, are you?" She begged him to be quiet, but he repeated the same statement. She said that Chris left, and they then went into the house. Kelly said, "I know what you're going to do. You're going to dump me for your fancy DA and give him all your money. You try and do that and make a public fool of me, and I'll make sure you never live to do it."

Ms. Baker then claimed that she thought about leaving the house again, but decided that this would just anger Kelly more, so she quietly went to her bedroom. She thought that Kelly might try and kill her, but she thought probably he would wait until she cut him out of the will or divorced him. She said that she was terrified; she locked her bedroom door and didn't sleep most of the night. She wondered if he would get one of the two guns they kept in the house. She said that both of the guns are hers, registered to her, and were given to her by her father, Elton Martin, who has an international corporation dealing in arms. She said that she kept the revolver in her room and said that Kelly had a gun in his room, which was the gun that he had when he threatened her.

The next day was the cook's day off. She got up sometime after 7:30 a.m. and went to the kitchen where she fixed a croissant, coffee, and juice. Around 8:00 a.m. she was sitting down at the kitchen table to eat when Kelly came in. He walked in, looked at her with an odd look, and pulled a pistol from his robe and told her he was going to kill her. He looked like he had been up all night drinking. He said a woman who plays around is immoral and unfaithful and has no right to live. She said that she realized she had to do something quickly and had to get control of the gun. She told Kelly that she had a letter that would prove that there was nothing to her relationship with McCormick and asked that he read it. She reached into the desk in the hallway and pulled out a letter from McCormick about the center. Kelly put the gun on the table and began reading the letter. She grabbed the gun. Kelly immediately swore and reached over to the kitchen counter and grabbed a large kitchen knife. She said he then yelled several obscenities and moved toward her. She yelled for him to stop, but he kept coming. He was holding the knife in his right hand, slashing it back and forth, and he cut her left arm several times as she tried to get out of his way. He then said something about it was now time to die, and she realized she only had one choice. She began to shoot and fired the gun until he dropped. She said Kelly dropped to the floor and made a few gurgling sounds and then was quiet. She could see blood all over the floor and on her arm and shoes. She didn't know what to do.

She then phoned Chris Spahn and asked Chris to come over immediately. She said Chris arrived about five minutes later, and Ms. Baker showed Chris what had happened. Chris then said that they had to call for help, and Sarah should call 911. Ms. Baker then called 911 and explained what happened, and the 911 operator told her not to touch anything, leave the gun in the house, get out of the house, and wait for the sheriffs to arrive. She and Chris did that.

I asked Ms. Baker whether she had ever fired guns before. She said that obviously she had some experience with guns, because her father was a major gun dealer, and she owned two guns. I asked if she had ever had to use one before. She said that other than her training in gun use and her periodic target training, the only incident was about one and a half years ago when she had to use one for protection on her property. She said that an irate former customer had come onto the grounds of Ashgate Farm around 7:30 in the evening and was yelling in front of her home. She went out and asked what was wrong, and the man said he had been cheated, that his pony had died, and called her a fraud. He said he wanted satisfaction right then. Ms. Baker said that she was frightened, as the man appeared to be headed for her front porch. She said that the only employee on the property was an incompetent drunk who did nothing, so she ran into her home, got the gun, and fired off several rounds in the air and told the man to leave. She said it worked, and the man ran down the road to his car and sped off. She said later she was issued a citation for improperly firing a weapon within an incorporated area. After conferring with her attorney, she decided to plead no contest and paid a $250 fine. I asked Ms. Baker who the incompetent employee was, and she said the first name was "Kit," but she didn't recall the last name.

I informed Ms. Baker that our department would continue our investigation and asked if she would give us permission to reenter her home for the purpose of conducting additional investigation, including seizing ammunition, looking for more blood spots, and examining correspondence. She said that she would not do that, as looking through her correspondence would invade her privacy. I told her that she had that right, and we would simply apply for a search warrant. I returned Ms. Baker to the jailer.

Search of Ashgate Home

At 1115 hours I contacted the on-call DA, Theresa Elliott, and informed her that our department needed to conduct additional investigation and that we would need a search warrant for the home. I explained the potential involvement of Mr. McCormick, and Ms. Elliott then informed me that this appeared to create a conflict for her office, and she was going to call the Attorney General's Office and ask them to handle the matter. She said someone from the AG's Office would call. I received a call at 1125 hours from Elton Voiselle of the AG's Office, who agreed to assist our office in obtaining a search warrant. A search warrant affidavit was prepared and presented to Judge Southworth, who issued the search warrant at 1320 hours. I then contacted criminalist Dale Ryan of the Darrow

County Crime Laboratory, who agreed to accompany me to the crime scene. Ryan and I arrived at Ashgate at 1345 hours.

I began the search by searching the upstairs bedroom in the north wing where Ms. Baker had gone to change her clothes. There on top of a closet shelf I found one gun, a .38-caliber Smith and Wesson revolver fully loaded, and a box of .38 ammunition. I also found a box of nine-mm ammunition that read 100 rounds and that contained 86 rounds. The top of the box was closed. I took custody of the .38 revolver and the ammunition and placed them in an evidence bag. In an antique desk in the corner of the room I found a document entitled, "Last Will and Testament of Sarah H. Baker." In reviewing the document, I noticed that Kelly Baker was listed as the principal beneficiary. I placed this document in an evidence envelope. Also, in the same desk in another drawer I found a handwritten letter sent with no envelope dated 8/14/05 that read:

> Dear Sarah,
>
> I know this is a tough grind, but we just have to get through it. Don't worry.
>
> It will all come out all right. Don't let it get you down.
>
> Brad

I placed this letter in an evidence envelope.

Ryan and I then went to a large upstairs bedroom in the south wing where we located clothing and articles of property of Kelly Baker. We did not locate any weapons or ammunition, and we did not see any alcoholic beverage in the room other than one small glass on a night table that appeared to have traces of whiskey. Next to the glass we found a small notepad with what appeared to be a list of items reading, "(1) D.A., (2) Restaurant, (3) House, (4) Will, (5) Divorce." Each of the five items were written in ink and item (5) was lined through in ink. There appeared to be a liquid stain that partially obscured the word "will." I seized the note as evidence.

Ryan and I then returned to the area of the kitchen. Ryan began taking measurements of the area where the body was located, where the kitchen chair and table were, the area where the casings and the gun were found, and areas where blood was located on the floor. Ryan pointed out what appeared to be a blood spatter on the east kitchen wall and a bloodstain on the chair. Ryan took samples of blood from the floor, the wall, and the chair and turned over custody of those samples to me for safekeeping. Ryan also extracted two bullets from the east wall, placed them in evidence envelopes, and turned them over to me for safekeeping.

I noticed that the kitchen table had a small plate with one croissant partially eaten, a full glass of orange juice, and one coffee cup partially full. I took custody of the cup, plate, and glass for possible fingerprint analysis. On the floor next to the table was a typed letter addressed to Sarah Baker from Chief Deputy District Attorney Bradley McCormick on District Attorney stationery that read:

> September 1, 2012
>
> Dear Ms. Baker:
>
> Your efforts in helping Darrow County develop a center for abused women have inspired volunteers and county workers. It is clear that under your able direction, our county will soon have a state-of-the-art facility to protect abused women and offer them a hope for their future.

Please accept the appreciation of our office and all the county agencies serving in Project WEB.

Sincerely,

Bradley W. McCormick

Chief Deputy District Attorney

I took custody of the letter and placed it in an evidence envelope.

Statement of Chris Spahn

At 1550 hours Forensic Scientist Ryan and I then drove to the home of Chris Spahn, which is located on the grounds of Ashgate Farm on Springs Road. Spahn agreed to speak with me and tell me what Spahn knew of the shooting. Spahn said that around 8:30 a.m. Sarah Baker called and said that something terrible had happened and asked Spahn to immediately come to the Ashgate residence. Spahn's home is about a quarter of a mile away. Spahn immediately ran over and found Sarah Baker standing on the front porch. She was shaking uncontrollably and crying. Spahn said that the two walked into the home and Sarah pointed to the kitchen and said, "He's in there. He's dead." Spahn walked into the kitchen and saw Kelly Baker lying on the floor. There was blood everywhere in the kitchen and on Sarah. Spahn said Sarah was bleeding from her arm. Spahn asked Sarah, "What happened?" Sarah told Spahn that Kelly was drunk and raging and tried to kill her with a knife, and she had to use the gun to defend herself. I asked Spahn what Sarah had said about where the gun was before she shot, and Spahn said that there was no mention of that.

Spahn was worried about Sarah and didn't know whether Kelly was dead, and Spahn said that they had to call 911 immediately. Sarah said she would do that, and Sarah placed the call. I asked Spahn how long the two took from the time Spahn arrived to when they called, and Spahn said about five minutes. I asked if Spahn saw any other weapons, and Spahn said only a knife in Kelly's hand, but Spahn did not look closely as Spahn was too shocked by the bloody scene and the confusion.

I asked Spahn what other information Spahn could offer, and Spahn said only that Sarah Baker was a wonderful person, and Sarah would only have shot Kelly if she truly believed she was going to be hurt or killed, as Sarah was a very kind and loving person.

On returning to the Detective Division, I stopped by the Coroner's Office, and, with the assistance of Dr. Sain, I obtained a blood sample and inked fingerprints from the body of Kelly Baker and Kelly Baker's robe and pajamas.

I retained all evidence for safekeeping, and when I completed all the fieldwork on September 7, I numbered each item of evidence and placed all the items in my personal locked evidence locker. The items that I booked for safekeeping were marked and are listed on the evidence sheet at the end of this report.

Recontact with Sarah Baker at County Jail

In light of the two letters that were recovered in the search and the delay in Sarah Baker's calling 911, I decided to talk further with Sarah Baker. At approximately 1700 hours I returned to the Darrow County Jail and asked to speak with Ms. Baker. The jailer brought Ms. Baker to the interview room. I explained that I wanted to ask some follow-up questions concerning evidence that I had located at her home and what appeared to be a delay in making the 911 call. Ms. Baker informed me that she had spoken with her attorney, who had advised her that she should not discuss the case further with law enforcement, and, therefore, she was unable to talk with me.

Statement of Bradley McCormick

At approximately 1730 hours I telephoned Bradley McCormick, the Chief Deputy District Attorney of Darrow County, by using the emergency county operator. Mr. McCormick was contacted in transit in his car, and he called me by cellular phone. I asked that he meet with me at the sheriff's station and informed him of my role in the investigation. Mr. McCormick said that he would meet me in about fifteen minutes.

At 1750 hours Mr. McCormick arrived at the station, and I spoke with him in my office. I informed Mr. McCormick of our investigation into the death of Kelly Baker. He said that he had already heard of Mr. Baker's death initially from Deputy District Attorney Theresa Elliott, and then others talked about it at the DA's office. I told him that Sarah Baker was a suspect, that she had been booked for murder, and that the Attorney General's Office was handling the prosecution. I said that his relationship with Sarah Baker was a matter of importance and told him that I needed to speak to him about that relationship. I said that I realized this might be personal, but that in view of statements that had already been made, it was imperative that I talk with him. He said that he would cooperate In any way possible.

Mr. McCormick said that his relationship with Sarah Baker was purely professional and stems from their working together to create a center for battered women through Project WEB and the Darrow County Battered Women Council. He said that there were numerous occasions when the two had to meet to work on plans for the center. Those meetings took place at Project WEB, at the meeting room of the council, and on occasion at Ashgate. He did not recall ever being completely alone with Sarah at Ashgate, and he couldn't remember the two of them eating alone at a restaurant. I asked Mr. McCormick if he had written Sarah. He said he was sure that he must have, but it would only have been about the center and Project WEB. I then showed McCormick the handwritten note dated August 14 that I had found in the Ashgate residence, and I asked him whether he had written it. McCormick paused for about ten seconds and then said, "Well, I forgot about that. It was just a note to Sarah to keep her spirits up. I asked him what he was referring to when he said, "I know this is a tough grind, but we just have to get through it." He said that he simply meant the tough process of getting the center approved and funded. He knew that at times it was discouraging for Sarah, because she was not used to this kind of political process.

I asked McCormick to let me know if he had any additional information that might be relevant to our investigation, and he assured me that he would. He then asked to what extent my department intended to release information about his professional relationship with Sarah to the press. I told him it was not up to me, and perhaps he should talk with Sheriff Litwhiler.

Request for Fingerprint Examination

At 0830 hours on September 8, 2012, I called Senior I.D. Technician Robin Mulligan of our department and requested that Mulligan conduct a fingerprint examination and comparison of evidence seized in this case. I informed Mulligan that Forensic Scientist Ryan would be conducting a full forensic scientific examination of many of the same items and, therefore, requested an early conclusion to Mulligan's examination so items could then be transferred.

Mulligan agreed to come to the Detective Division immediately. At 0840 hours I turned over to Mulligan items of evidence # 1–9 and 17–27.

Statement of Kit Manville

At 0950 hours on September 8, 2012, I called Chris Spahn and asked if the employment records revealed any employees at Ashgate Farm with the first name of Kit. Spahn informed me that for a period of two years Ashgate employed a Kit Manville as a farrier. Spahn said that Manville was terminated on September 1, 2012, by Spahn's action after conferring with Sarah Baker. The grounds entered in the employment records were, "Lack of competence and dependability." Spahn said that Manville was not punctual and did not complete shoeing jobs on time. Spahn said that Manville was given three months' severance pay. Although there were no separate entries in the employment records about Manville's failure to complete jobs on time and Manville's tardiness, Manville had been "talked to" about the problem. There was one previous entry by Spahn concerning work performance on April 18, 2011. Sarah Baker had reported to Spahn that a week or two previous she had seen Manville intoxicated and felt that should be entered in Manville's employment record. Spahn said that Manville was capable of doing very good work, and Manville was an asset as an entertainer when they had parties, but Manville had a big problem with "the bottle." Manville was kept on because Mr. Baker and Manville were friendly. Finally, the problem got too severe, and Manville had to be discharged.

I asked Spahn for Manville's address and phone number. Spahn informed me that Manville lived at 19925 Talbot Road in the county and gave me Manville's phone number. I then phoned Manville and made arrangements to go to Manville's home for an interview.

At 1140 hours on September 8, 2012, I drove to Manville's residence. Manville informed me that Manville was employed by Ashgate Farm as a farrier in March 2010. Manville had extensive experience as a farrier, and because of Manville's experience dealing with polo ponies with the Barrett Farm, Manville was recruited with the promise of more pay and more side opportunities to provide singing entertainment for Ashgate parties. Manville has for a number of years sung and played guitar for upscale parties. Manville first met with Chris Spahn, and after Spahn made the decision to hire Manville, then Manville met with Ms. Baker and Manville was hired.

Manville said problems began when Manville had the misfortune to witness an incident involving Ms. Baker. Manville said that a customer named Will White bought a polo pony from Ashgate Farm and later the pony died. White thought that Ashgate knew or should have known of the illness, and when Ashgate claimed the pony was fine when sold, White became angry. Manville said White talked with Spahn about the problem, and Spahn said they were not responsible. Apparently White then asked who was Spahn's boss, and Spahn said that Ashgate Farm was owned by Ms. Baker. White came by in the evening about 7:00 p.m. and apparently couldn't find anyone. Manville happened to be completing some work and talked with White. White said that he left messages for Ms. Baker and she would not return his calls, so he came by to talk to her. He asked where her home was, and Manville indicated it was down the road. White walked down to the house, and Manville walked along to make sure everything was all right. He saw them talking on the porch, and then Ms. Baker yelled for him to leave. White walked down from the porch and stood at the bottom of the steps and said something about suing Ms. Baker. He said Ms. Baker again yelled for him to leave and then went into the house. She came out about one minute later and had a gun in her hand. She pointed it up in the air and yelled, "You get out of here now, unless you want to be carried out!" Without another word, she began firing the gun in the air. White ran to his car and left.

Ms. Baker came down the steps to Manville and said, "You saw what he did. He tried to attack me." Manville just gave a shrug of the shoulders, and Ms. Baker then went back in the house. Apparently White called the sheriff, because about one hour later two deputies arrived. They saw Manville working and asked what Manville saw. Manville repeated to the deputies what happened. About one week later Ms. Baker's lawyer called Manville and said that she understood Manville was going to be a witness for the prosecution. Manville told the attorney the same thing Manville told the sheriffs and said that was all Manville knew. Manville denied drinking alcohol that day at work and only had a drink after going home that evening.

Manville said that Mr. Baker was a great guy and was always very friendly and helpful to Manville. Mr. Baker would come home some evenings, and if Manville was still working at the farm, they would talk and sometimes have a beer. Sometime several months ago Manville began to think that Ms. Baker was getting pretty cozy with a good-looking guy who was always coming to the house for "meetings." This bothered Manville, because Mr. Baker was never there when this happened. One evening Mr. Baker came home, and apparently Ms. Baker was gone. He came over to Manville, and they had a beer or two. After talking for a while, Manville decided to see if Mr. Baker knew anything about this new man, so Manville mentioned the meetings. Manville said that Mr. Baker said he was sure it was just business dealings with the battered women project.

Then one evening around 6:30 p.m. Manville saw Ms. Baker and this guy get out of Ms. Baker's Lexus and walk to the front porch. He heard Ms. Baker say something like, "Oh, Brad, I love the things you say to me." Then Ms. Baker put her head next to the man's shoulder and just laughed. They walked into the house. Mr. Baker must have had a late news broadcast, because he didn't come home while Manville was there. Manville said the two then came out of the house about an hour later. They got in her Lexus and drove off.

About one week later Manville was at the farm office, heard Ms. Baker and Chris Spahn talking in the next office, and heard Ms. Baker say, "I've decided to cut Kelly out of the will." The next day Manville called Kelly Baker at KNTA and told him what had happened. Apparently Kelly Baker was shocked, because there was a long pause, and then Kelly Baker said, "You're a true friend, and I won't forget it."

Shortly after that Chris Spahn gave Manville a termination notice with three months' severance pay. That was the last Manville heard about the matter until the news broke on TV that Kelly Baker had been murdered and his wife had been arrested. Manville said that Sarah Baker must have murdered him to get him out of the way so that she could marry the guy she was so cozy with. Manville was "annoyed and upset" that Ms. Baker would let Manville go and thought the termination was a "big sham" just to get rid of Manville. Manville "hoped that Ms. Baker rotted in jail."

Manville admitted that in years past Manville had alcohol problems and still was on probation for drunk driving.

Receipt of Evidence from Coroner

At 1300 hours I went to the Coroner's Office and received from Dr. Sain two bullets that had been removed from the body of Kelly Baker. I marked each separately as item # 31 and item # 32 and placed them in evidence envelopes in my evidence locker.

Release of Custody of Evidence to Forensic Scientist Ryan

At 1345 hours on September 8, 2012, at the request of Forensic Scientist Ryan, I retrieved items # 10–16 and items 28–34 from my locked evidence locker to deliver these items directly to Ryan at the Crime Laboratory so that Ryan could complete a full forensic scientific examination of all relevant items of evidence.

Receipt of Evidence from Forensic Scientist Ryan

On September 10, 2012, I was informed by phone that Forensic Scientist Ryan had concluded the forensic scientific examination of the evidence in this case. At 1130 hours I went to the Crime Laboratory and received items 1–34 from Ryan. I returned to the Detective Division and placed these items in my locked evidence locker for potential future evidentiary use.

Review of Police and Sheriff's Records on Kelly Baker and Sarah Baker

I ran automated records checks on Kelly Baker and Sarah Baker. I found two police entries for Kelly Baker, a battery arrest in 2008 and a DUI in 2009. I found one sheriff's entry for Sarah Baker, a citation for CC 12031 in 2011. I contacted the police and sheriff's records custodians and obtained official copies for each offense and have attached them to this report.

Items of Evidence

Item 1 One nine-mm Luger semiautomatic pistol, serial #6851

Item 2 One butcher knife

Item 3 Two nine-mm cartridge cases

Item 4 One nine-mm cartridge case

Item 5 One nine-mm cartridge case

Item 6 Four nine-mm cartridges, 6a from chamber and 6b, 6c, and 6d from magazine

Item 7 Six .38-caliber cartridges

Item 8 One .38-caliber Smith and Wesson revolver

Item 9 One pair of white canvas sneakers

Item 10 One hair sample from Sarah Baker

Item 11 One sealed vial of blood from Sarah Baker

Item 12 One pair of slacks from Sarah Baker

Item 13 One blouse from Sarah Baker

Item 14 One blood sample from the kitchen floor

Item 15 One blood sample from the kitchen wall

Item 16 One blood sample from the kitchen chair

Item 17 One glass from the kitchen

Item 18 One plate with croissant from the kitchen

Item 19 One cup from the kitchen

Item 20 One typewritten letter

Item 21 One handwritten letter

Item 22 One document entitled, "Last Will and Testament of Sarah Baker"

Item 23 One note and notepad

Item 24 One box of nine-mm ammunition

Item 25 One box of .38-caliber ammunition

Item 26 Inked fingerprints of Sarah Baker

Item 27 Inked fingerprints of Kelly Baker

Item 28 One sealed vial of blood from Kelly Baker

Item 29 One men's robe from Kelly Baker

Item 30 One pair of men's pajamas from Kelly Baker

Item 31 One nine-mm bullet from wound #1 received from Dr. Sain

Item 32 One nine-mm bullet from wound #3 received from Dr. Sain

Item 33 One nine-mm bullet from kitchen wall 31" high received from Dale Ryan

Item 34 One nine-mm bullet from kitchen wall 33" high received from Dale Ryan

NITA CITY POLICE DEPARTMENT
OFFENSE REPORT

FILE NUMBER: 08–12117

VICTIM: Sally Johnson

SUSPECT: Kelly Baker

LOCATION: Cooney's Irish Pub
29 Plaza Walk
Nita City, Nita

OFFENSE: CC 242—Battery

REPORT: May 3, 2008

BY: Officer Morgan Culler, # 88 *mCC*

DETAILS OF OFFENSE

At 2245 hours I was patrolling the Plaza Walk area when I heard yelling coming from Cooney's Pub. I ran inside the bar and saw a man and a woman standing near the bar. The man was swearing and the woman was crying. I separated the two and could see that the man appeared to be under the influence of alcohol. I directed the man to sit at a table and then talked to the woman. The woman gave me her name as Sally Johnson. She said she was the cocktail waitress, and she had mistakenly removed a glass from the man's table and he became irate. When he discovered his glass was gone, he walked over to her, grabbed her by the arm, and yelled at her, "Where the hell is my drink?" She told him the drink was empty, and he shoved her against the wall yelling, "Don't you pull that stuff on me." She said that I arrived immediately after that happened. The bartender, Sheldon Fetzer, confirmed Ms. Johnson's account.

I then returned to the man involved in the incident. He gave me his name as Kelly Baker and told me that he worked for KNTA-TV. He said that he had joined KNTA about one year ago and was on the news team. He asked that I drop the matter, as it wouldn't be a very popular thing for the Nita Police to arrest a television personality. I told Mr. Baker that I would be happy to listen to his side of the story, but that witnesses had already confirmed that he had used profanities and roughly handled Ms. Johnson. Baker said that this bar was obviously "a dive," and they made their money by using tactics like removing their drinks before they were finished. I told Baker that he had a choice. Either he could leave the bar, in which case I would issue him a citation, or he could refuse, and I would arrest him and take him to jail. He said he would take the citation and leave. Ms. Johnson and Mr. Fetzer said they would appear as witnesses if necessary, and they could be reached at Cooney's. I issued the citation.

NITA CITY POLICE DEPARTMENT
OFFENSE REPORT

FILE NUMBER: 09–17434

OFFENSE: CC 23152—DUI

DATE AND TIME: July 13, 2009 at 0145 hours

BY: Officer Melinda Rowell, # 167   *MR*

DETAILS OF OFFENSE

On July 13, 2009, at 0145 hours I was working swing DUI shift in a marked DUI vehicle proceeding eastbound on Rosecrans Blvd. west of Fulton St. I saw a Mercedes convertible southbound on Fulton turn left to go westbound on Rosecrans. The Mercedes screeched the tires making the turn, passed me, and proceeded westbound straddling the dividing line between the two Rosecrans westbound lanes. I made a U-turn at Fulton and then followed the Mercedes for about six blocks. The Mercedes came to a stop at the intersection of Moore St. even though there was no signal or stop sign at that intersection and no vehicles crossing the intersection. The Mercedes then slowly moved westbound in the right lane. I activated the overhead warning lights and followed. When the Mercedes did not stop, I activated the siren. The Mercedes slowly pulled over to the curb, parking the right front wheel slightly over the curb.

I approached the driver, who was alone, and asked him for identification. He had difficulty getting his wallet and then produced a Nita driver's license #J3559791 in the name of Kelly Baker. I recognized Mr. Baker from his television news appearances. I asked him where he was going, and he said home. I asked him where he was coming from, and he said there had been a little staff celebration because he was going to become a news anchor. Mr. Baker's speech was slurred, he smelled of some alcoholic beverage, and I told him that I was going to have to ask him to perform some sobriety tests. He pleaded with me, asking that I just take him home and forget the matter. I told him I could not do that. He said that he didn't want to "take any stupid goddamn tests" and said I had better let him go or my "job was on the line." I told him that he could either take the tests or I would have to take him downtown and arrest him. I then demonstrated the heel-to-toe test and asked him to take it. Mr. Baker took two or three steps and then fell to the side and said he didn't want to take any more tests. I then placed Mr. Baker under arrest, handcuffed him, and placed him in the back of my patrol car. I secured his 2009 Mercedes-Benz SL500 roadster convertible and called a tow truck to take it to the impound lot. I then transported Mr. Baker to the Darrow County Jail. I informed Mr. Baker of his rights to a blood, breath, or urine test. Mr. Baker agreed to take a breath test. The breath test was administered in the prescribed manner, and Mr. Baker blew a .17 and a .18. He was then booked in the County Jail.

DARROW COUNTY SHERIFF'S OFFICE
OFFENSE REPORT

FILE NUMBER: 11–04331

VICTIM: William H. White

SUSPECT: Sarah Baker

LOCATION: Ashgate Farm, 8714 Springs Road, Warrenton, Nita

OFFENSE: CC 12031—Discharge of Firearm in Unincorporated Area

DATE: April 10, 2011

BY: Deputy Marian Bracken, # 344   *MB*

At 1935 hours I was patrolling the east Warrenton area when I received a call from dispatch of a shooting at Ashgate Farm reported by victim. I responded to the Shell station at Springs Rd. and Gulliver Blvd., and at 1942 I spoke with victim. He said that he had gone to Ashgate to discuss a problem he had when he boarded his pony at the farm and the pony died. When he arrived at the farm he spoke with someone named Kit. He gave up talking to Kit as Kit appeared to be somewhat affected by alcohol, so he went to the main house and knocked on the door. The woman who answered was Sarah Baker, the owner of Ashgate. She refused to talk to him and ordered him off the property. She left, came back with a gun, and said she would kill him. He ran to his car. As he got about 100 feet away he heard shots, but doesn't know where the shots went. He demanded that Ms. Baker be arrested for assault with a deadly weapon.

At 2015 hours I arrived at Ashgate Farm and spoke with Sarah Baker. She was agitated, at times crying, and claimed that the victim had come to her home, began yelling in front of her home, and when she went out he threatened her. She ran to get a gun to protect herself. I asked her to explain the threat, and the victim said, "If you don't give me the money you owe me, I'll burn your house down with you in it." After she got the gun, the victim started to leave, turned around and said something, and she thought he was going to come back and hurt her. She fired the gun in the air twice, and he then turned and ran off. The only reason she used the gun was she had no protection. The only other person nearby was an employee named Kit Manville, who takes care of the horses. She called Manville, but Manville was obviously drunk and wouldn't come to her aid. I checked the weapon, a nine-mm Luger, serial #6851, and found four live rounds in the magazine and one in the chamber. I found three expended nine-mm casings, two on the porch and one at the foot of the porch steps. I contacted Kit Manville, who appeared to be UI alcohol. Manville heard the shots, but claimed not to have heard any of the conversation. I issued a citation to Sarah Baker for a violation of CC 12031, as it is illegal to fire a weapon in that area of the county unless in self-defense. I did not confiscate the weapon as Ms. Baker admitted firing the same.

DARROW COUNTY SHERIFF'S DEPARTMENT
BUREAU OF FORENSIC SCIENCE REPORT

FILE NUMBER:	12–28088
SUSPECT:	Sarah Hanna Baker 8714 Springs Road Warrenton, Nita
LOCATION:	Ashgate Farm 8714 Springs Road Warrenton, Nita
OFFENSES:	CC 187—Murder
DATE OF REPORT:	September 10, 2012
BY:	Forensic Scientist Dale Ryan *DR*

Search of Ashgate Farm Residence

Per the request of dispatch, on September 7, 2012, at approximately 1325 hours, I contacted Detective Holmes, who informed me that I was needed to assist in an investigation of a shooting at Ashgate Farm in Warrenton. I met Detective Holmes at the station, and we drove to Ashgate Farm, arriving at approximately 1345 hours. Detective Holmes had a search warrant and knocked at the front door. No one answered, and Detective Holmes used a key to open the front door. We entered the home and went directly to the upstairs bedroom, which was obviously occupied by Sarah Baker, as we saw only women's clothing. Detective Holmes then searched for and located one gun and some ammunition. We then went to the other side of the house and searched Kelly Baker's bedroom. There Detective Holmes seized a notepad with writing and a handwritten letter.

We then went to the first-floor kitchen, and I measured distances from Kelly Baker's body (position shown to me by Detective Holmes) to the kitchen table, chair, the position of the nine-mm pistol and the casings (again shown to me by Detective Holmes), and bloodstains on the floor, chair, and wall. I also measured the height and width of the table and the chair. I took samples of blood from the spot on the floor in front of the sink, from the chair, and from the blood spatter on the wall. I placed the items in sealed evidence containers. I retrieved two bullets from the east wall, one 31" in height and the other 33" in height. I placed them in sealed evidence envelopes. Lying on the floor near the table was a typewritten letter, which Detective Holmes seized. I did not see any evidence of blood on the kitchen table.

At the conclusion of our examination of the residence at Ashgate, Detective Holmes and I then drove to the home of Chris Spahn, arriving there sometime around 1600 hours. Following our discussion with Spahn, I turned over to Detective Holmes for safekeeping the blood samples and bullets I retrieved from the kitchen area.

Examination of the Body and Clothing of Kelly Baker

At 1650 hours I went to the Darrow County Coroner's Office and performed a gunshot residue test on the body of Kelly Baker. I found no traces of primer residue on the body of Kelly Baker.

Preparation of Diagrams

At 0815 hours on September 8, 2012, I prepared an elevation sketch of kitchen furniture and diagrams of the kitchen, the Ashgate home, and Ashgate Farm.

Custody of Items of Evidence

At 1015 hours on September 8, 2012, I received a call from Senior I.D. Technician Robin Mulligan that Mulligan had concluded a fingerprint examination of twenty items of evidence that had been turned over to Mulligan by Detective Holmes. Approximately one-half hour later I went to the Bureau of Identification and received directly from Mulligan the twenty items of evidence that bore the markings given them by Detective Holmes of Items # 1–9 and 17–27.

I then contacted Detective Holmes by telephone at 1330 hours and asked Det. Holmes to deliver the remaining items of evidence in the case. Detective Holmes delivered items of evidence bearing markings "Items 10–16" and "Items 28–34." I began my examination of the evidence in this case at approximately 1400 hours on September 8, 2012, and concluded my examination on September 10, 2012, at 0930 hours.

Blood Examination

Results

Item 2   Test results indicate the presence of blood in three stained areas, designated A, B, and C, on the knife from the right hand of Kelly Baker. Stain A is located on the tip area of the knife blade, on the side of the knife designated A. Stain B is located near the tip area of the knife blade, on the side of the knife designated B. Stain C is located on the handle.

Human deoxyribonucleic acid (DNA) was isolated from the stain designated A from the knife. This sample was amplified and typed at the HLA DQA1 locus and the PM system. Refer to the table for the typing results of this sample. No further testing was conducted on the stain designated A at this time.

No DNA isolation or amplification results at the HLA DQA1 locus and the PM system were obtained for the stain designated B from the knife. Therefore, no determination can be made as to the possible origin of this stain.

Human DNA was isolated from the stain designated C from the knife. This sample was amplified and typed at the HLA DQA1 locus and the PM system. Refer to the table for the typing results of this sample. No further testing was conducted on the stain designated C from the knife at this time. No evidence of hairs, fibers, or apparent tissue was noted on this item.

Item 9   Test results indicate the presence of blood in five stained areas, designated A through E, on the shoes from Sarah Baker. Stain area A is located on the instep side of the right shoe on the canvas and foxing. Stain areas B and C are located on the bottom (outsole) area of the right shoe. Stain area D is located on the bottom (outsole) area of the left shoe. Stain area E is located on the instep side of the left shoe on the foxing.

Human DNA was isolated from the stains designated A and B from the shoes. These samples were amplified and typed at the HLA DQAl locus and the PM system. Refer to the table for the typing results of these samples. No further testing was conducted on the stains designated A and B from the shoes at this time.

No DNA isolation or amplification results at the HLA DQA1 locus and the PM system were obtained from the stains designated C, D, and E from the shoes. Therefore, no determination can be made as to the possible origin of these stains. Test results also indicate the presence of blood on the toe area of the right shoe, additional areas on the bottom (outsole) of the right shoe, the outstep of the left shoe on the foxing, and additional areas on the bottom (outsole) of the left shoe. No further testing was conducted on these stained areas at this time.

Item 11   No alcohol, morphine, cocaine, benzoylecgonine, cannabinoids, acidic or neutral drug, or other alkaline extractable drugs were detected. Human DNA was isolated from the blood sample of Sarah Baker. This sample was amplified and typed at the HLA DQA1 locus and the PM system (which includes the LDLR, GYPA, HBGG, D7S8, and GC loci). Refer to the table for the typing results of this sample.

Item 12   Test results indicate the presence of blood on the exterior left front thigh area of the slacks from Sarah Baker. No DNA isolation or amplification results at the HLA DQA1 locus and the PM system were obtained for this sample. Therefore, no determination can be made as to the possible origin of this stain.

Item 13   Test results indicate the presence of blood in four stained areas, designated A through D, on the blouse from Sarah Baker. Stain A is located on the exterior right rear arm seam about one inch from the end of the sleeve. Stain area B is located on the interior left rear sleeve. Stain area C is located on the interior hem of the right rear side. Stain area D is located on the interior right front sleeve.

Human DNA was isolated from the stains designated A, B, C, and D from the blouse. These samples were amplified and typed at the HLA DQA1 locus and the PM system. Refer to the table for the typing results of these samples. No further testing was conducted on the stains designated A, B, C, and D from the blouse at this time.

Item 14   Test results indicated the presence of blood on the swab from the floor in front of the sink in the kitchen. Human DNA was isolated from this swab. The sample was amplified and typed at the HLA DQA1 locus and the PM system. Refer to the table for the typing results of the sample. No further testing was conducted on this item at this time.

Items 15 and 16   Test results indicated the presence of blood on the swabs from the blood spatter on the wall and from the chair in the kitchen. Human DNA was isolated from these swabs. The samples were amplified and typed at the HLA DQA1 locus and the PM system. Refer to the table for the typing results of these samples. In an effort to determine whether Item 15 contained any saliva, I administered an amylase mapping or overlay test. That test revealed no saliva present. No further testing was conducted on these items at this time.

Item 28 No morphine, cocaine, benzoylecgonine, cannabinoids, acidic or neutral drug, or other alkaline extractable drugs were detected. **Sample contained blood alcohol .08 percent by weight.** Human DNA was isolated from the blood sample of Kelly Baker. This sample was amplified and typed at the HLA DQA1 locus and the PM system. Refer to the table for the typing results of this sample.

Item 29 Test results indicated the presence of blood in two stained areas, designated A and B, on the robe from Kelly Baker. Stain area A is located on the exterior right rear area from the center back to just below the waistline. Stain area B is located on the exterior right and left front area just below the waist.

Human DNA was isolated from the stained areas designated A and B on the robe. These samples were amplified and typed at the HLA DQA1 locus and the PM system. Refer to the table for the typing results of these samples.

Item 30 Test results indicated the presence of blood in three stained areas, designated A, B, and C, on the pajamas from Kelly Baker. Stain area A is located on the exterior right rear of the pants below the waistband. Stain area B is located on the exterior right and left front of the pants just below the waist and extending down the thigh area. Stain area C is located on the pajama top in the center rear back area to the bottom of the pajama top.

Human DNA was isolated from the stained areas designated A, B, and C on the pajamas. These samples were amplified and typed at the HLA DQA1 locus and the PM system. Refer to the table for the typing results of these samples.

Conclusions

Based on the above typing results, the DNA profile obtained from the stain area designated A on the shoes from Sarah Baker, located on the instep side of the right shoe (Item 9), the stained swab from the floor in front of the sink in the kitchen (Item 14), and the stain areas designated B, C, and D located on the interior of the blouse from Sarah Baker (Item 13) is consistent with the DNA profile of Sarah Baker and different from the DNA profile of Kelly Baker. Therefore, Sarah Baker cannot be eliminated as a possible contributor to the genetic material isolated from these samples. Kelly Baker is eliminated as a possible contributor of this genetic material.

The DNA profile obtained from the stain area designated B on the shoes from Sarah Baker, located on the bottom (outsole) of the right shoe (Item 9), the stained swabs from the wall and the kitchen chair (Items 15 and 16), the stain designated A located on the exterior right rear arm seam of the blouse from Sarah Baker (Item 13), the stain area designated C located on the handle area of the knife found in Kelly Baker's hand (Item 2), the stain areas designated A and B on the robe from Kelly Baker (Item 29), and the stain areas designated A, B, and C from the pajamas from Kelly Baker (Item 30) is consistent with the DNA profile of Kelly Baker and different from the DNA profile of Sarah Baker. Therefore, Kelly Baker cannot be eliminated as a possible contributor of the genetic material isolated from these samples. Sarah Baker is eliminated as a possible contributor of this genetic material.

The DNA profile obtained from the stain area designated A on the tip area of the blade of the knife found in Kelly Baker's hand (Item 2) is consistent with a mixture of the DNA profiles of Sarah Baker and Kelly Baker. Therefore, neither Sarah Baker nor Kelly Baker can be eliminated as possible co-contributors of this genetic material.

No conclusive typing results were obtained on the stain areas designated C, D, and E on the shoes from Sarah Baker (Item 9), on the stain area from the slacks from Sarah Baker (Item 12), or on the stain area designated B from the tip of the knife found in Kelly Baker's hand (Item 2). Accordingly, no determination can be made as to the possible origin of the genetic material isolated from these samples.

Blood spatter on the wall measured at forty-two to forty-six inches from the floor. This fact and the **bloodstain on the chair led me to conclude that Mr. Baker was seated when he was shot. The blood** spatter was consistent with a medium to high-velocity gunshot. The absence of saliva in the sample indicates that the spatter was not the result of aspiration.

The presence of Kelly Baker's blood on the handle of the knife and the coroner's finding that there was blood on Kelly Baker's right palm leads me to conclude that the knife was placed in Kelly Baker's hand after he was shot and not, as Sarah Baker claimed, in his hand when he allegedly attacked her. Also, the absence of Kelly Baker's blood on the knife blade except for stain area A is inconsistent with Ms. Baker's claim of a knife attack. Blood spatter and blood droplets would be expected on the knife blade under such a factual scenario.

As to the other items of evidence listed above, I was unable to detect any evidence of blood for purposes of either visual observation or testing.

Firearms Examination

Results

Examination of Item 1 pistol revealed it to be a World War II vintage nine-mm Luger pistol, serial number 6851, in mechanical operating condition with the safety features functioning properly.

Examination of Item 8 revolver revealed it to be a Smith and Wesson .38-caliber double-action revolver, serial number F017052, in mechanical operating condition with the safety features functioning properly.

The Remington-Peters nine-mm Luger cartridge cases, Items 3, 4, and 5, and the nine-mm Luger jacketed bullets, Items 31–34, were identified as having been fired by the Item 1 pistol.

The Remington-Peters nine-mm Luger cartridge, Item 6a, was identified as having been loaded into and extracted from the Item 1 pistol.

The Remington-Peters nine-mm Luger cartridges, Item 24, are the types designed for use with a firearm such as the Item 1 pistol. The cartridges are the same type and brand as the Items 3, 4, and 5 cartridge cases, and Items 6a–d cartridges, and they are loaded with jacketed bullets similar to Items 31–34 bullets.

Examination of Items 29 and 30, the robe and pajamas of Kelly Baker, reveal holes consistent with entrance bullet holes in the right shoulder and right upper chest. Additionally, there are three holes in the back; holes consistent with right-to-left grazing entrance and exit in the right back and a separate exit hole in the left back. Microscopic and chemical examination of the areas surrounding the bullet holes failed to reveal residues suitable for accurate muzzle-to-garment distance determinations.

Examination of the pants of Item 30, the pajamas of Kelly Baker, failed to reveal any bullet holes or visible gunshot residues.

I test-fired Item #1, the nine-mm Luger pistol, shooting targets from a variety of distances. I found that gunpowder residue was left from a muzzle to target distance of four feet or less. Therefore, I concluded that the gun Sarah Baker fired must have been more than four feet from Kelly Baker's body at the time of firing.

Conclusions

Based on the location of the blood spatter at forty-two to forty-six inches from the floor, the presence of blood on the kitchen chair consistent with that of Kelly Baker, the location of the two bullets recovered from the wall, one at thirty-one-inch height and the other at thirty-three-inch height, the positions of the two bullets recovered from the body of Kelly Baker, my use of a Styrofoam dummy to reconstruct the trajectory of the bullets, and the DNA and amylase analysis of the blood spatter and chair stain consistent with the blood of Kelly leads me to conclude that Kelly Baker was seated when he was shot. The blood spatter was consistent with a medium to high-velocity gunshot.

Release of Evidence to Detective Holmes

On September 10, 2012, at approximately 1135 hours at the Crime Laboratory, I turned over items 1–34 to Detective Holmes for safekeeping.

I certify that I performed the above analyses and examinations as an employee of and in a laboratory operated by the Bureau of Forensic Science and that the above is an accurate record of the results of those analyses and examinations.

Dale Ryan

Forensic Scientist

SUMMARY TABLE OF HLA DQA1 AND PM TYPING RESULTS

ITEM	DESCRIPTION	HLA DQA1	LDLR	GYPA	HBGG	D7S8	GC
11	Blood Sample from Sarah Baker	1.2, 1.2	AB	AB	AA	AB	AC
28	Blood Sample from Kelly Baker	4.1, 4.2/4.3	AB	BB	BB	BB	AC
2	Knife from K. Baker—stain area A	1.2 (dominant), (4.1), (4.2/4.3)	AB	AB	A(B)	AB	AC
2	Knife from K. Baker—stain area B	INC	INC	INC	INC	INC	INC
2	Knife from K. Baker—stain area C	4.1, 4.2/4.3	AB	BB	BB	BB	AC
9	Shoes from Sarah Baker—stain area A	1.2, 1.2	AB	AB	AA	AB	AC
9	Shoes from Sarah Baker—stain area B	4.1, 4.2/4.3	AB	BB	BB	BB	AC
9	Shoes from Sarah Baker—stain area C	INC	INC	INC	INC	INC	INC
9	Shoes from Sarah Baker—stain area D	INC	INC	INC	INC	INC	INC
9	Shoes from Sarah Baker—stain area E	INC	INC	INC	INC	INC	INC
12	Slacks from Sarah Baker	INC	INC	INC	INC	INC	INC
13	Blouse from Sarah Baker—stain area A	4.1, 4.2/4.3	AB	BB	BB	BB	AC
13	Blouse from Sarah Baker—stain area B	1.2, 1.2	AB	AB	AA	AB	AC
13	Blouse from Sarah Baker—stain area C	1.2, 1.2	AB	AB	AA	AB	AC
13	Blouse from Sarah Baker—stain area D	1.2, 1.2	AB	AB	AA	AB	AC
14	Swab from floor in front of sink	1.2, 1.2	AB	AB	AA	AB	AC
15 &16	Swabs from wall and from kitchen chair	4.1, 4.2/4.3	AB	BB	BB	BB	AC
29	Robe from Kelly Baker—stain areas A and B	4.1, 4.2/4.3	AB	BB	BB	BB	AC
30	Pajamas from Kelly Baker—stain areas A–C	4.1, 4.2/4.3	AB	BB	BB	BB	AC

Notes: Numbers and/or letters in parentheses () represent alleles present in lesser intensity than other alleles not in parentheses.

INC indicates inconclusive results.

DARROW COUNTY SHERIFF'S DEPARTMENT
BUREAU OF IDENTIFICATION REPORT

FILE NUMBER: 12–28088

SUSPECT: Sarah Hanna Baker
                 8714 Springs Road
                 Warrenton, Nita

OFFENSE: CC 187—Murder

DATE OF REPORT: September 11, 2012

BY: Senior I.D. Technician Robin Mulligan

On September 8, 2012, at 0830 hours, I received a telephone request from Detective Lee Holmes asking that I conduct a fingerprint examination and comparison of evidence seized in the above case. Detective Holmes informed me that the evidence would soon be turned over to Forensic Scientist Dale Ryan and asked that I perform my examination as soon as possible. I then went to the Sheriff's Detective Division and at 0845 hours received from Detective Holmes twenty items of evidence labeled Items #1–9 and 17–27.

On September 8, 2012, at 1030 hours, I conducted my examination of the items of evidence as follows:

Photographing of Evidence

Before conducting any fingerprint examination I photographed Item #1, the nine-mm Luger pistol, serial #6851, and magazine, and Item 2, the butcher knife.

Item #1—Nine-mm Luger Pistol and Magazine

I examined Item #1 and found it to be a nine-mm Luger pistol, serial #6851, with a magazine. I processed Item 1 for prints and was able to find one usable latent on the trigger guard of the pistol, which I lifted and labeled Latent #1. There were other partial prints in the area of the trigger guard and on the clip that appeared smudged and unusable. I then compared Latent #1 with the prints in Items 26 and 27 and was able to find sufficient points of comparison to state that Latent #1 was left by the right index finger of Sarah Baker.

Item #2—The Butcher Knife

After checking both the blade and the handle, I was unable to find any usable prints.

Items #3–9

After checking these items, I was able to find one usable print on the side of Item #6b. As I understand it, this live cartridge was found in the magazine of the nine-mm pistol. I labeled this Latent #2 and compared it with the known inked impressions in Items 26 and 27. I was able to positively identify Latent #2 as a print made by the right index finger of Kelly Baker.

I was able to find one usable latent print on Item #8 on the .38-caliber revolver cylinder. I lifted that print and labeled it Latent #5. I then compared it with the known prints In Items 26 and 27 and found it to be the right thumb of Sarah Baker.

Items #17–19

I processed these items for prints and was able to find two usable latent prints. I found one latent print on Item #17, the glass, approximately one inch below the top with print horizontal to the top edge of the glass and the print pointing from left to right. I labeled that Latent #3 and compared it with Items 26 and 27 and was able to find sufficient points of comparison to state that Latent #3 was made by the right index finger of Sarah Baker. The second latent print was found on Item #18, the plate, on the underside. I lifted that and labeled it Latent #4. I compared it with the prints in Items 26 and 27 and found it to be the left index finger of Kelly Baker.

Items #20–23

No usable prints were detected in examining these items.

Items #24–25

I processed these items for prints and was unable to find any usable latent prints. I returned Latents #1–#5 to my evidence locker. I then called Det. Holmes at approximately 1450 hours on September 8, 2012, and informed Det. Holmes of the results.

RELEASE OF EVIDENCE TO FORENSIC SCIENTIST DALE RYAN

On September 8, 2012, at 1038 hours, Forensic Scientist Ryan came to the Bureau of Identification, and I turned over to Ryan each of the evidentiary items, Items 1–9 and 17–27, for Ryan's forensic scientific examination.

Coroner of Darrow County

Gross Autopsy Record

Case Title: In re Kelly Lawrence Baker—Darrow County Sheriff's Department

Pathologist: Morgan P. Sain, MD   Autopsy No.: 12–1826

Patient: Kelly L. Baker   Sex: Male   Age: 34   Ht.: 72"   Wt.: 170

Eyes: Brown   Hair: Brown   Mustache: No   Beard: No

Autopsy At: Coroner's Office, 44 Van St., Nita City   Time: 8:25 a.m.   Date: 09/08/12

Initial Investigation

At 8:55 a.m. on September 7, 2012, I received a call from Deputy Coroner Clem Beazley informing me that there had been a suspected homicide at Ashgate Farm in the county. Deputy Coroner Beazley met me at the Coroner's Office, and we drove to Ashgate Farm, arriving at 9:35 a.m. Detective Holmes of the Sheriff's Department escorted us into the kitchen area. There I saw the body of an adult male identified to me as Kelly Baker, who was lying facedown on the kitchen floor. There was blood on the floor and on Kelly Baker's face, chest, right arm, and back. His body was still warm to the touch. Detective Holmes informed me that there was a knife in Kelly Baker's right hand when Holmes first arrived, but Holmes took possession of the knife and placed it in an evidence bag. I examined Kelly Baker's right hand and noticed that the palm area and the anterior surfaces of the fingers were covered with blood. While I was at Ashgate Farm, I saw Sarah Baker. She had several superficial cuts to her left arm. I found those curious, as none appeared to be serious, and they did not even require bandaging. They appeared in my opinion to be self-inflicted.

The body of Kelly Baker revealed apparent multiple gunshot wounds. There did not appear to be any other evident trauma visible. Deputy Coroner Beazley made arrangements to place the body of Kelly Baker in a body bag and transport the body to the Coroner's Office.

At 4:30 p.m. Detective Holmes contacted me at the Coroner's Office and requested the opportunity to take a full set of fingerprints and a blood sample from the body of Kelly Baker. I accompanied Holmes to the morgue where Holmes took a full set of inked fingerprint impressions, and I took a vial of blood from the body of Kelly Baker. The robe and pajamas were removed from the body of Kelly Baker. Detective Holmes took possession of these items.

Report of Autopsy

Pathological Diagnosis

1. Penetrating gunshot wound with entrance on right side of face and injury to right carotid artery.

2. Perforating gunshot wound with entrance on right upper chest, injury to pulmonary artery trunk, heart and lungs, bilateral hemothoraces, and exit from lateral left thorax.

3. Penetrating gunshot wound with entrance on the lateral right shoulder and injury to soft tissue and bone.

4. Perforating gunshot wound with entrance on right back, injury to soft tissue, and exit from right back.

Cause of Death

Gunshot wounds of neck and thorax.

General Description and External Examination

Rigor: Complete   Livor: Reddish   Distribution: Posterior

This is the body of a well-developed and nourished male. The body was in a body bag. Paper bags were over the hands. Fingerprint ink was on the fingertips. The body was unclothed. There were no personal effects. There was a 12-cm scar on the lower back. There were no tattoos. There was no external evidence of medical intervention. The external evidence of trauma consisted exclusively of gunshot wounds (see below). No other external evidence of trauma was found. The fingernails were short and intact.

Gunshot Wounds

1. Penetrating gunshot wound with entrance on right side of face at 8" below the top of the head and 3-3/4" to the right of the midline; 1/4 × 3/16" irregular round wound with 1/16" marginal abrasion ring; no evidence of powder debris. The wound track passes backward, downward, and leftward, perforating the right common carotid artery and soft tissue of the neck and back. A large caliber bullet with a deformed side was recovered in the subcutaneous tissue of back at 10" below the top of the head and 1-1/4" to the right of the posterior midline.

2. Perforating gunshot wound with entrance on right upper chest at 13" below the top of the head and 2-3/4" right of the midline; 3/16" round wound with a 1/16" marginal abrasion ring and singeing of the right lateral margin, 1/8". The wound track passes backward, downward, and leftward, perforating the right second intercostal space, the right upper and lower lung lobes, the pulmonary arteries trunk to the lateral left ventricle of the heart, the left upper and lower lung lobes and the left lateral six intercostal space to exit the lateral left back at 18" below the top of the head and 9" left of the posterior midline through a 3/8 × 1/4" oval wound.

3. Penetrating gunshot wound with entrance on the lateral right shoulder at 10" below the top of the head and 7-1/4" to the right of the anterior midline; 3/16" round wound with a 1/16" marginal abrasion ring; no evidence of powder debris. The wound track passes backward, downward, and leftward, perforating and fracturing the head of the humerus, perforating soft tissue of the chest wall, and the body of cervical vertebra number five. The wound track continues perforating and fracturing the left clavicle and terminates in the left shoulder just anterior to the head of the left humerus, where a large caliber jacketed bullet with a deformed side was recovered at 12-1/2" below the top of the head and 7" to the left of the midline.

4. Perforating gunshot wound with entrance on right back at 18-1/2" below the top of the head and 4" right of the midline; 3/8 × 1/4" oval wound with lateral guttering, 1 × 3/8". The wound

track passes downward, and leftward, perforating soft tissue of back to exit the right back at 18-5/8" below the top of the head and 2" to the right of the midline through a 1/2 × 3/8" oval wound with a medial guttering, 1-1/4 × 1/2".

Internal Examination

The body is opened with the usual Y-shaped incision. The organs of the thoracic and abdominal cavities are in their normal anatomic positions.

Pleura and Pericardium

Missile wound track; bilateral hemothoraces, partially clotted blood, approximately 75 ml right and 1000 ml left.

Peritoneum

Intact, smooth, and glistening.

Heart

350 gm. Right ventricle, three mm; left ventricle, thirteen mm. No valvular or congenital abnormalities. Coronary arteries, normal origin and distribution; right coronary artery predominant; left anterior descending, right coronary artery and left circumflex, no significant sclerosis all segments. Myocardium, missile wound track involving pulmonary artery trunk and left ventricle; no gross evidence of inflammation or fibrosis. Aorta, no significant alteration.

Lungs

Right 310 gm; left 230 gm. Hyoid bone, no evidence of trauma. Larynx, trachea, and bronchi intact and free of trauma or obstruction. Lungs, missile wound track of right upper and lower lobes and left upper and lower lobes; no evidence of inflammation or pulmonary artery emboli. Hemidiaphragms intact.

Liver

1405 gm. Capsule intact and smooth; parenchyma, no evidence of trauma, inflammation, or fibrosis.

Gallbladder

No significant alteration.

Spleen

65 gm. Capsule intact; parenchyma, no significant alteration.

Pancreas, Thyroid Gland, And Adrenal Glands

No significant alteration.

G.I. Tract

Esophagus, stomach, small and large intestine, no evidence of trauma, hemorrhage, or ulceration. Appendix present. Stomach contains approximately 120 ml of creamy, tan fluid with soft tan food fragments.

Kidneys

120 gm each. Capsules strip with ease revealing intact, smooth cortical surfaces; parenchyma, no evidence of trauma or inflammation.

Urinary Bladder

Wall intact, contains approximately 20 ml of clear yellow urine.

Genitalia

Prostate and testes, no significant alteration.

Head

The scalp is reflected following an intermastoid incision, and the calvarium is removed. Scalp and skull, no evidence of trauma. Cerebral meninges and brain, no evidence of trauma, hemorrhage, or inflammation; brain, 1370 gm. Cerebrospinal fluid, clear. Circle of Willis, no significant alteration.

Skeletal System

No evidence of trauma except along missile wound tracks.

Microscopics

Sections of skin taken from the entrance wounds labeled #1, #2, #3, and #4 are negative for powder debris. Sections of pulmonary artery, heart, and lung taken from along missile wound tracks reveal hemorrhage and tissue disruption. Sections of liver show no significant alteration.

Toxicology Report

Name: Kelly Lawrence Baker   Date: 09/10/12

The blood was screened by Forensic Scientist Dale Ryan of the Crime Laboratory for morphine, cocaine, benzoylecgonine, cannabinoids, acidic or neutral drugs, or other alkaline extractable drugs. None was detected. The blood was also screened for alcohol and was determined to be .08 percent by weight. **For more details including DNA analysis see the Crime Lab report by Dale Ryan.**

X-Rays

(6) X-Rays of the head, thorax, and abdomen show the bullets (2) in the neck and thorax.

Summary

The deceased was shot by an assailant.

Cause of Death

Gunshot wounds of neck and thorax.

Disposition of Evidence

Vial of blood to Detective Holmes on 09-07-12 at 4:30 p.m. Two bullets to Detective Holmes on 09-08-12 at 1:00 p.m. Body and clothing to Metropolitan for Triner Funeral Home on 09-09-12 at 9:30 a.m.

Morgan P. Sain

Morgan P. Sain, MD
Medical Examiner and Forensic Pathologist
Darrow County
Nita City, Nita 99995
Dictated 09/10/12
Signed 09/11/12

BODY DIAGRAM

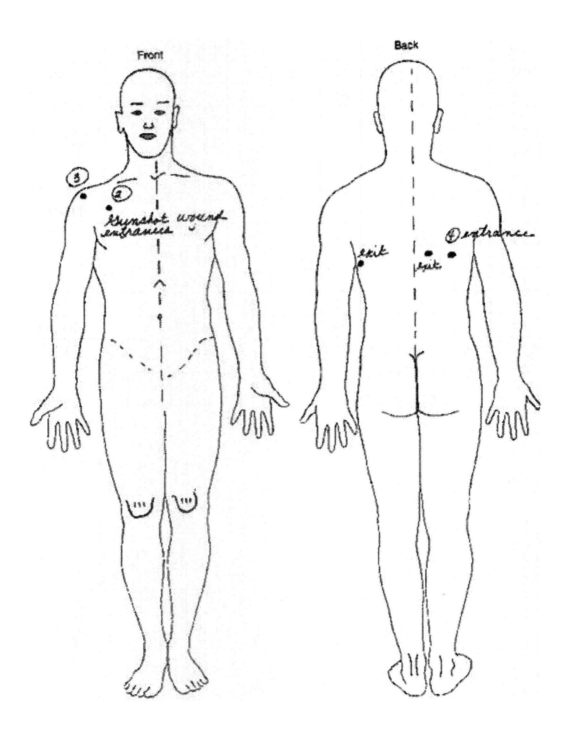

Decedent's Name: Kelly Lawrence Baker

Examined By: Morgan P. Sain, MD

Date: 9/8/2012

BODY DIAGRAM—HEAD—KELLY BAKER

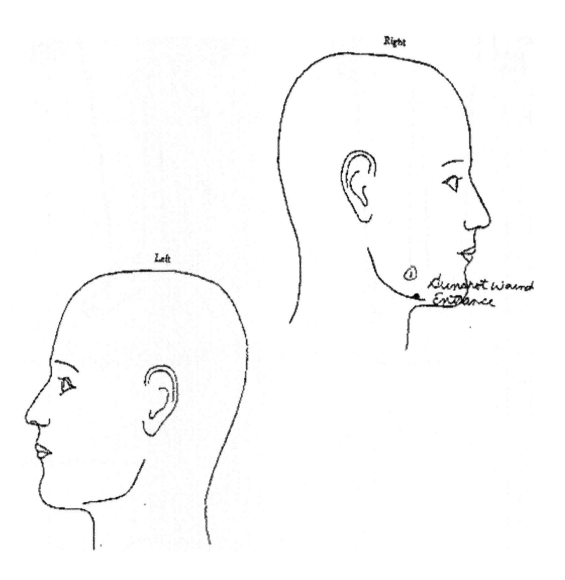

Decedent's Name: Kelly Lawrence Baker

Examined By: Morgan P. Sain, MD   Date: 9/8/2012

GUNSHOT WOUND CHART

		Wound No.							
		1		2		3		4	
		Ent	Bullet	Ent	Exit	Ent	Bullet	Ent	Exit
1. Location of Wound	Head								
	Neck	X							
	Chest			X					
	Abdomen								
	Back				X			X	X
Arm	Right					X			
	Left								
Leg	Right								
	Left								
2. Size of Wound	Diam.			3/16		3/16			
	Width	3/16			1/4			1/4	3/8
	Length	1/4			3/8			3/8	1/2
3. Inches from Wound to:	Top of head	8	10	13	18½	10	12½	18½	18-5/8
	Right of midline	3¾	1¼	2¾		7¼		4	2
	Left of midline				9		7		
4. Powder Debris	On skin								
	Clothing								
5. Direction of Bullet Through Body	Backward	X		X		X			
	Forward								
	Downward	X		X		X		X	
	Upward								
	To right								
	To left	X		X		X		X	
6. Bullet Found	Caliber	X		NO		X		NO	

Name: Kelly Lawrence Baker

Examined By: Morgan P. Sain, MD

City or County: Nita

Date: 9/8/2012

DIAGRAM OF SARAH BAKER'S LEFT ARM CUTS

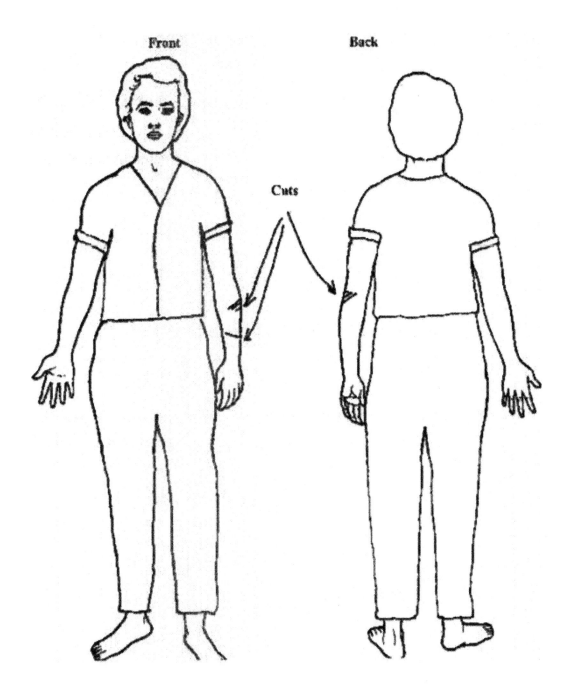

Examined By: Morgan P. Sain, MD   Date: 9/7/2012

HANDWRITTEN LETTER FOUND IN DESK

8/14/2012

Dear Sarah,

I know this is a tough grind,

but we just have to get through it.

Don't worry. It will all come

out all right. Don't let it get

you down.

Brad

Typed Letter Found in Kitchen

OFFICE OF

THE DISTRICT ATTORNEY

NITA CITY OFFICE DARROW COUNTY
550 Main Street
Nita City, Nita 55055

WARRENTON OFFICE
1359 Johnson Blvd.
Warrenton, Nita 55060

ELLEN T. FORREST DISTRICT ATTORNEY

September 1, 2012

Sarah H. Baker
Ashgate Farm
8714 Springs Road
Warrenton, Nita 55060

Dear Ms. Baker:

Your efforts in helping Darrow County develop a center for abused women have inspired volunteers and county workers. It is clear that under your able direction, our county will soon have a state-of-the-art facility to protect abused women and offer them a hope for their future.

Please accept the appreciation of our office and all the county agencies serving in Project WEB.

Sincerely,

Bradley W. McCormick

Bradley W. McCormick

Chief Deputy District Attorney

BWM:et

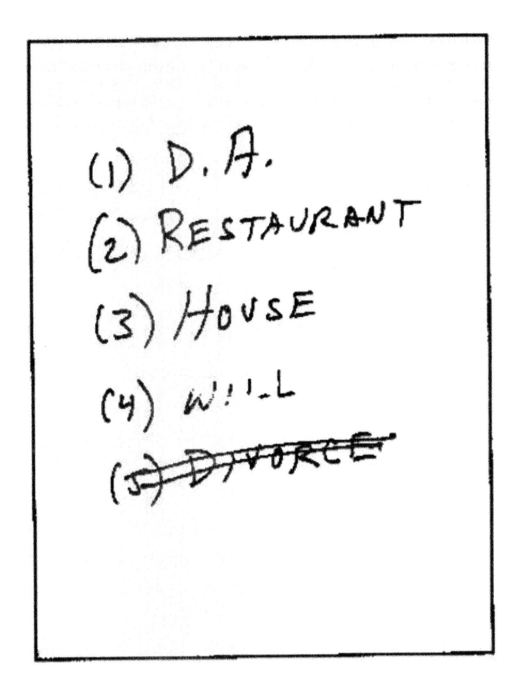

Last Will and Testament of Sarah Baker

I, Sarah Hanna Baker, a resident of the County of Darrow, State of Nita, declare that this is my last will.

FIRST: I revoke all former wills and codicils to wills.

SECOND: Kelly Baker, my husband, is living. I have no children or issue of any deceased child.

THIRD: I have not entered into a contract to make a will or a contract not to revoke a will.

FOURTH: If my husband survives me by thirty days, I give all my property to him except for the residence and land located at 8718 Springs Road in Warrenton.

FIFTH: If my husband does not survive me by thirty days, I give all of my property to my father, Elton Martin, except for the residence and land located at 8718 Springs Road in Warrenton.

SIXTH: I give the residence and land located at 8718 Springs Road in Warrenton to Chris Spahn, the manager of Ashgate Farm.

SEVENTH: I appoint my husband executor of this will, to serve without bond; and, if he fails or ceases so to act, I appoint my father, Elton Martin, as the executor of this will, to serve without bond.

EIGHTH: I authorize my executor, with or without notice, to sell at either public or private sale all property belonging to my estate, subject only to such confirmation of court as may be required by law.

NINTH: If any beneficiary under this will directly or indirectly contests or attacks this will or any provision thereof, the gift to that beneficiary is revoked, and the property that would have been given to that beneficiary shall be distributed as though that beneficiary had predeceased me without issue.

IN WITNESS WHEREOF, I have subscribed this will, consisting of these two pages, at the end thereof on this 24th day of March, 2009.

Name: *Sarah Hanna Baker*

Subscribing Witnesses: *Lisa Williams*
Ashley S. Patterson

On this date and in our presence, Sarah H. Baker, the testatrix, personally subscribed her name at the end of the foregoing instrument, at which she declared to us, as attesting witnesses, that it was her will; at the request of the testatrix and in her presence and in the presence of each other, we have subscribed our names as witnesses to her will; at that time, the testatrix was over eighteen years of age and appeared to be of sound mind; we have no knowledge of any facts indicating that the instrument, or any part of it, was procured by duress, menace, fraud, or undue influence.

We, individually, certify under penalty of perjury that the foregoing is true and correct. Executed on this 24th day of March, 2009, at Nita City, Nita.

Lisa Williams

residing at 1142 High Street
Nita City, Nita

Ashley S. Patterson

residing at 302 Greenup Street
Nita City, Nita

SEARCH WARRANT

IN THE DISTRICT COURT
OF THE STATE OF NITA
COUNTY OF DARROW

THE STATE OF NITA	)
	) Case No. SW-106–12
In re Sarah Baker	)
	)
	)

X   To Det. Holmes of the Darrow County Sheriff's Dept.

You are hereby commanded in the name of the State of Nita to forthwith search either in day or night the residence at 8714 Springs Road, Warrenton, Nita, described as a single-family dwelling of red brick and stone construction on Springs Road off Route 211 in Darrow County, for any firearms, ammunition, knives, blood, fingerprints, correspondence in any way relating to the death of Kelly Baker and any necessary measurements and diagrams.

You are further commanded to seize said property, person, and/or objects if they be found and to produce before this court an inventory of all property, persons, and/or objects seized.

This search warrant is issued in relation to an offense substantially described as follows:

The murder of Kelly Baker in violation of Section 187 of N.C.C. I, the undersigned, have found probable cause to believe that the property or person constitutes evidence of the crime identified herein or tends to show that the person(s) named or described herein has committed or is committing a crime and further that the search should be made, based on the statements in the attached affidavit sworn to by

Det. Lee Holmes

Name of Affiant Date and Time

September 7, 2012 at 1:20 p.m.

Kevin McClintock

Magistrate

SEARCH WARRANT INVENTORY AND RETURN

IN THE DISTRICT COURT
OF THE STATE OF NITA
COUNTY OF DARROW

THE STATE OF NITA   )
) Case No. SW-106–12

In re Sarah Baker   )
)
)

The following items, and no others, were seized under authority of this warrant:

1. One Smith and Wesson .38-caliber revolver.
2. One box .38-caliber ammunition.
3. One box nine-mm Luger ammunition.
4. One note from a notepad.
5. One handwritten letter from Brad.
6. One typewritten letter from Bradley McCormick.
7. One Last Will and Testament of Sarah Baker.
8. Measurements from the kitchen.
9. One blood swab from the chair in the kitchen.
10. One blood swab from the wall in the kitchen.
11. One blood swab from the floor in the kitchen.
12. One cup.
13. One glass.
14. One plate with croissant.
15. Two bullets from east wall of the kitchen.

The statement above is true and accurate to the best of my knowledge and belief.

September 7, 2012   Lee Holmes

Date   Executing Officer

Subscribed and sworn before me this day

September 7, 2012   Kevin McClintock

Date   Magistrate

ARREST AND CONVICTION RECORD OF SARAH HANNA BAKER

RE: WRIGHT, E. NAG DATE: 09-09-12 TIME: 1630
CIR/C7184544
SEX/F
NAM/01 BAKER, SARAH HANNA
NAM/02 MARTIN, SARAH HANNA
NDL/J2558782
SOC/696329331

****

ARR/DET/CITE/CONV:

#1

04-10-11 CIT. DCSO CC 12031-DISCHARGE OF FIREARM IN PROHIBITED AREA
04-17-11 CONVICTED, MISDEMEANOR CC 12031-DISCHARGE OF FIREARM IN PROHIBITED AREA, FINE $250.

NOT TO BE DUPLICATED

ARREST AND CONVICTION RECORD OF KELLY LAWRENCE BAKER

RE: WRIGHT, E. NAG DATE: 09-14-12 TIME: 1505
CIR/D4973134
NAM/01 BAKER, KELLY LAWRENCE
NDL/J3559791
SOC/893314496

****

ARR/DET/CITE/CONV:

#1

05-03-08 CIT. NCPD CC 242-BATTERY, MISDEMEANOR
05-24-08 PLED NO CONTEST TO MISDEMEANOR DISTURBING THE PEACE, 6 MONTHS
SUMMARY PROBATION, $200 FINE

****

#2

07-13-09 ARREST NCPD CC 23152-DUI, MISDEMEANOR
08-08-09 PLED GUILTY TO MISDEMEANOR DUI, 3 YEARS PROBATION, 2 DAYS
COUNTY JAIL, $750 FINE

NOT TO BE DUPLICATED

ARREST AND CONVICTION RECORD
OF KIT MANVILLE

RE: WRIGHT, E. NAG DATE: 09-11-12 TIME: 1458

CIR/B7653449

NAM/01 MANVILLE, KIT

NDL/N7024377-SUSPENDED UNTIL 01-17-09

SOC/535667984

PROBATION: EXP: 01-17-15 CC 23152-DUI WITH TWO PRIORS

****

ARR/DET/CITE/CONV:

#1

07-08-05 ARREST NCPD CC 11357(b)-POSSESSION OF MARIJUANA, MISDEMEANOR

07-20-05 PETITION SUSTAINED, JUVENILE COURT, WARDSHIP

09-09-05 VIOLATION OF PROBATION, REVOKED, 5 DAYS JUVENILE HALL

****

#2

09-02-07 ARREST DCSD CC 537c-LIVERYMAN FRAUDULENT ANIMAL LOAN, MISDEMEANOR

09-09-07 CONVICTED, PLEA OF GUILTY, CC 537c, 5 DAYS COUNTY JAIL, SUSPENDED, INFORMATION PROBATION 1 YEAR, FINE $100, RESTITUTION

****

#3

11-10-08 ARREST NCPD CC 23152-DUI, MISDEMEANOR

11-22-08 CONVICTED, PLEA OF GUILTY, MISDEMEANOR DUI: SEN. 3 YEARS FORMAL PROBATION, 2 DAYS COUNTY JAIL, FINE $750

04-27-10 VIOLATION OF PROBATION, REVOKED & REINSTATED, 15 DAYS COUNTY JAIL

****

#4

04-03-10 ARREST NHP CC 23152-DUI, MISDEMEANOR

04-27-10 CONVICTED, PLEA OF GUILTY, MISDEMEANOR DUI W/PRIOR: SEN. 3 YEARS
FORMAL PROBATION, 30 DAYS COUNTY JAIL CONCURRENT, FINE $1,500

01-17-12 VIOLATION OF PROBATION, REVOKED, 90 DAYS COUNTY JAIL
CONCURRENT

****

#5

12-02-11 ARREST NHP CC 23152-DUI, MISDEMEANOR

01-17-12 CONVICTED, JURY TRIAL, MISDEMEANOR DUI W/2 PRIORS: SEN. 3 YEARS
FORMAL PROBATION, 90 DAYS COUNTY JAIL, $2,000 FINE

NOT TO BE DUPLICATED

ARREST AND CONVICTION RECORD OF CHRIS SPAHN

RE: WRIGHT, E. NAG DATE: 09-16-12 TIME: 1505

CIR/B9428731

NAM/01 SPAHN, CHRIS

NDL/F7882929

SOC/551422876

****

ARR/DET/CITE/CONV:

#1

03-13-07 ARREST NSPD CC 484-EMBEZZLEMENT, FELONY

03-15-07 RELEASED FROM CUSTODY, VICTIM REFUSED TO PROSECUTE

****

#2

10-25-09 ARREST NSPD NITA EMPLOYMENT CODE(NEC) §1320-DIVERSION OF EMPLOYMENT BENEFITS, MISDEMEANOR

11-14-09 CONVICTION, MISDEMEANOR NEC 1320, 2 YEARS PROBATION, RESTITUTION, FINE $1,500

NOT TO BE DUPLICATED

TESTIMONY OF DETECTIVE LEE HOLMES AT PRELIMINARY HEARING[1]

DIRECT EXAMINATION

1 My name is Lee Holmes. I am a detective with the Darrow County Sheriff's Department. I have
2 been employed by the department for eleven years. I have served in the Custody Division for
3 two years, five years in Patrol, one year in Internal Affairs, and three years in Detectives. During
4 those years I have worked a variety of cases including homicides, robberies, burglaries, other crimes
5 of theft, and crimes against the person, such as assaults, batteries, child molestation, and rapes.
6
7 On September 7 of last year I was working the day shift. At 8:52 a.m. I was at the station prepar-
8 ing a report when I got a call on my mobile radio from Dispatcher Karl to respond to a homicide
9 at Ashgate Farm just outside Warrenton. Karl informed me that Deputy Camelli was in the area
10 and would secure the scene. I left immediately and arrived about eighteen minutes later. Deputy
11 Camelli was already at the scene, and I took over handling the case.
12
13 When I arrived, Deputy Camelli was standing outside the home with the defendant and with
14 the Ashgate manager, Chris Spahn. I was informed by Deputy Camelli that she had fully secured
15 the residence, checking to make sure no one else was in the house. She informed me that she
16 found the body of the defendant's husband, Kelly Baker, lying facedown in the kitchen. She said
17 that she checked for vital signs and found none. She called the Coroner's Office, as the defendant
18 had told her the shooting had taken place more than forty-five minutes earlier.
19
20 I entered the home and found that Deputy Camelli's observations were correct. I saw Kelly
21 Baker's body lying facedown. There was a large amount of blood in his area. He was holding a
22 butcher knife in his right hand. There was a nine-mm Luger pistol in the kitchen along with four
23 empty nine-mm cartridges lying on the floor near the refrigerator. I took custody of the knife, the
24 pistol, serial number 6851, with a live round in the chamber and three in the magazine, and the
25 empty cartridges and placed them in separate evidence envelopes.
26
27 I then walked back outside to the front porch where the defendant was being detained by
28 Deputy Camelli. I noticed that she appeared unusually calm, although she was talking to Deputy
29 Camelli about her arm wounds. I looked at her left arm and noticed what appeared to be several
30 minor cuts or scratches with a slight amount of blood. I noticed that she had blood on her blouse
31 and on her white sneakers.
32
33 I contacted Dispatcher Karl by radio and asked Karl to relate for me the conversation Karl had
34 with the defendant when she first called the Sheriff's Department. Based on the conversation,

---

[1] The transcript of Detective Lee Holmes's testimony was excerpted so that only Detective Holmes's answers are reprinted here. Assume that this is a true and accurate rendering of Detective Holmes's answers. The testimony was given at the preliminary hearing on October 20, 2012, in the Darrow County Municipal Court, Nita City, Nita.

1   which Dispatcher Karl said would be transcribed and made a part of the record of the investiga-
2   tion report, and based on my observations at the scene, I placed the defendant under arrest for the
3   murder of her husband. The defendant then asked if she could change her shoes. I escorted her
4   upstairs to her bedroom and watched her take off the sneakers and put on a different pair. I then
5   took possession of the sneakers and placed them in an evidence envelope.
6

7   The Coroner's Office personnel arrived and took custody of Kelly Baker's body. I then trans-
8   ported the defendant to the Darrow County Jail for booking. While there I asked that the medical
9   staff examine the defendant to see what her medical condition was. Nurse Alex Nelson, in my
10   presence, examined the defendant's left arm and cleaned the cuts. They did not require any further
11   medical attention. Nurse Nelson, at my direction, obtained both blood and hair samples from the
12   defendant and gave them to me in separate vials. Nurse Nelson then took the defendant behind a
13   screened area, gave the defendant a pair of standard-issue jail overalls, and handed me the defen-
14   dant's bloody blouse and her trousers. I placed them in separate evidence bags.
15

16   Throughout the time the defendant was in my custody, including the time later when I took a
17   full statement from her, she at no time displayed any emotion other than expressing a concern over
18   her wounds to her left arm. She at no time expressed any remorse for her husband's death. All she
19   seemed concerned about was when she was going to be bailed out.
20

21   We obtained a search warrant from Judge Southworth to search the Ashgate residence and exe-
22   cuted that warrant later that afternoon with Darrow County criminalist Dale Ryan at approximately
23   1:45 p.m. During the search in the second-story bedroom where the defendant changed shoes,
24   I located a .38-caliber Smith and Wesson revolver that was fully loaded with six rounds. It was on a
25   shelf in a closet. Immediately next to it was a closed box of .38-caliber ammunition containing ninety-
26   four of the original 100 rounds. Next to that box was a closed box of nine-mm Luger ammunition
27   containing eighty-six of the original 100 rounds. I placed the revolver and the two ammunition boxes
28   in separate evidence bags, which I retained. The clothing in the closet was all women's clothing.
29

30   Because the warrant authorized seizing relevant correspondence, I searched an old desk in the
31   other corner of the same bedroom and found a document entitled, "Last Will and Testament of
32   Sarah Baker." In a separate drawer of the desk I located a handwritten letter addressed to the defen-
33   dant and signed "Brad." Later, in searching the kitchen I found on the floor near Mr. Baker's body
34   a typed letter addressed to the defendant from Bradley McCormick. I placed all three documents
35   in separate evidence envelopes.
36

37   In the second-floor south wing I searched a bedroom containing personal effects of Kelly Baker.
38   There were no weapons of any kind or ammunition in the room. On the night table next to
39   the bed there was a notepad. The top sheet listed five items, which were, "D.A.," "Restaurant,"
40   "House," "Will," and "Divorce." The last item had a line drawn through it.
41

42   Throughout the search I was accompanied by Dale Ryan. When we returned to the first floor,
43   Ryan proceeded to take measurements of the kitchen area and took samples of blood from the
44   floor, the chair, and the wall. I pointed out to Ryan a plate, a glass, and a cup on the table, and
45   I took custody of those items for possible fingerprinting.

1   The entire search of the premises took about two hours. We then drove to the residence occu-
2 pied by Chris Spahn, who is the farm manager. We were there approximately twenty minutes, and
3 sometime around 4:15 p.m., I retained all the items of evidence I had secured in the search until
4 September 8 when I turned certain items over to Senior I.D. Technician Mulligan and others over
5 to Forensic Scientist Ryan. On September 10, Forensic Scientist Ryan returned all items to me.
6 I have retained them for safekeeping since that date.

Cross-Examination

1   The defendant was cooperative at all times from the time that I first encountered her outside
2 Ashgate until I had concluded my initial interview of her at the jail. She did not refuse to talk to
3 me either at the scene or during the initial jail interview. I recall that when I advised her of her
4 *Miranda* rights, she said that she understood she didn't have to talk to me, but she said she wanted
5 me to know what happened. When I asked her if we could search her home, she said that she had
6 no objection to our looking for anything except correspondence. The reason she gave was that she
7 thought everybody had a right to privacy concerning their own letters.
8
9   I did not contact any other people who worked for Ashgate Farm to see if anyone else witnessed
10 the defendant and Bradley McCormick when they were on the property. I did not check to see if
11 any maids, cooks, or groundskeepers were on the property the day that Kit Manville claimed to
12 have seen them enter the house. I did not talk to anyone else who might have been present at The
13 Saddle Restaurant when the two had dinner. I did not conduct interviews of others who were pres-
14 ent for meetings of the Battered Women Council or Project WEB as to how the two conducted
15 themselves when they were both at those meetings. I did not contact workers or former workers
16 of Kit Manville to see what they would say about Manville's character for truth and honesty or
17 Manville's feelings toward the defendant.
18
19   I did not search some of the other rooms to see if there were firearms or ammunition located
20 elsewhere in the house. I did check our department records to see what firearm was used by the
21 defendant in the April 10, 2011, incident, and I noted that she was issued a citation. Apparently
22 no firearm was ever booked as evidence. Therefore, I cannot say whether she used a .38-caliber
23 revolver on that occasion.
24
25   I did not check with Kelly Baker's friends, people he worked with, or former employers to deter-
26 mine what his character for violence was. I did locate two Nita Police Department reports that
27 revealed a battery and a DUI conviction, but I did not check to see whether police records in areas
28 where he had previously lived and worked showed any arrests or convictions. I understand that he
29 previously worked for a TV station in Nevada. I believe it was in Las Vegas. I do know from work-
30 ing cases both as a detective and as a patrol officer that some people who are ordinarily law abiding
31 and peaceful can become combative and assaultive when they are drinking.
32
33   I did not check Kelly Baker's hands when I found him on the floor. As I understand it, the only
34 people who touched the body after Deputy Camelli arrived were Deputy Coroner Clem Beazley
35 and the autopsy surgeon Dr. Sain. I have no personal knowledge whether there was or was not
36 blood on the palm of Mr. Baker's right hand.

1   I did find a glass next to the notepad on the night table in Mr. Baker's bedroom. There was a
2   small amount of liquid in the glass, and it did smell like whiskey. In addition, there was a spot on
3   the note over item number 4. The spot did not look like blood, and it could well have been from
4   the liquid in the glass. I am aware that Mr. Baker's toxicology study showed that he had a blood
5   alcohol level of .08 percent, but I wouldn't express an opinion about how much he could have had
6   earlier. That would be up to a criminalist.
7
8   I am aware that sometimes people who have to fight to defend themselves go into a shock-like
9   state afterward and don't show any emotion for some time. I have seen that once or twice. I have
10   also seen relatives of people who were killed delay their reactions because of shock. But I can tell
11   you that I haven't seen anyone accused of killing someone who was any cooler than the defendant
12   was that morning.
13
14   It is true that the defendant had what looked like cuts on her left arm, and there did appear to
15   be a small amount of blood several places on her upper and lower left arm.

I hereby certify that the foregoing is a true and correct transcription of the testimony of Detective Lee Holmes on October 20, 2012, at the preliminary hearing in *State v. Baker*, in the Darrow County Municipal Court, Nita City, Nita.

Certified by:

Julian Lanfranconi

Julian Lanfranconi
Court Reporter

TESTIMONY OF DR. MORGAN SAIN AT PRELIMINARY HEARING[2]

DIRECT EXAMINATION

1   I hold a medical degree and am a pathologist and director of the Pathology Laboratory of the
2   Darrow County Coroner's Office here in Nita City. I have been a pathologist with that office
3   since 2006. I graduated from Tufts University with a BS in Biology in 1991. I received an MS
4   in Biology at Southern Methodist University in 1993. In 1999 I earned a PhD in Experimental
5   Pathology and an MD at Case Western Reserve University. I was a resident in Anatomic and
6   Clinical Pathology at Duke University Medical Center from 1999 through 2002. I then served
7   as an assistant chief medical examiner in Chapel Hill, North Carolina, for one year as part of a
8   forensic pathology fellowship. I then became a forensic pathologist with the Diagnostic Pathology
9   Medical Group in Nita City. In 2006 I accepted a position as assistant director of Pathology at the
10   Darrow County Coroner's Office. Five years later I was appointed as the director. I have taught
11   pathology at Nita University Medical School from 2004 through 2009. I am board certified in
12   three fields of pathology: anatomical, clinical, and forensic. I also sit regularly on the certification
13   board of the American Board of Pathology as an examiner of applicants for board certification.
14
15   I have testified in state and federal trial courts in this state and in North Carolina and given
16   expert testimony in the field of forensic pathology on approximately 130 occasions. On most such
17   occasions I was called by the prosecution, but in at least fifteen or sixteen cases I was called to tes-
18   tify as a defense witness. As a member of the medical staff of the Coroner's Office I am employed
19   by Darrow County. I also am a member of the Nita Clinical Laboratory and am assistant chief of
20   the Department of Pathology at Salk Hospital, both private institutions.
21
22   In the course of my work in North Carolina, Diagnostic Pathology Medical Group, and the
23   Darrow County Coroner's Office, I have performed approximately 3,000 autopsies, around
24   25 percent of which were classified as gunshot deaths. I qualified as an expert and testified in court
25   and rendered opinions with respect to gunshot death cases on more than thirty occasions. I have
26   lectured in the field of gunshot wound deaths before groups of doctors, police officers, and medical
27   staffs of hospitals and have taken part in professional group discussions in this area.
28
29   On September 7, 2012, I was informed at the Darrow County Coroner's Office by Deputy
30   Coroner Beazley that there had been a shooting at Ashgate Farm just outside of Warrenton. The
31   two of us drove to Ashgate, arriving there sometime around 9:30 a.m. I was escorted inside the
32   house to the kitchen area. There I saw the body of Kelly Baker. It was obvious that Mr. Baker had
33   been dead for at least an hour. Mr. Baker was lying facedown on the floor. I checked and found no
34   pulse, his body was still slightly warm, and there was blood on his face, his right arm, and on the

---

[2] The transcript of Dr. Morgan Sain's testimony was excerpted so that only Dr. Sain's answers are reprinted here. Assume that this is an accurate rendering of Dr. Sain's answers. The testimony was given at the preliminary hearing on October 20, 2012, in the Darrow County Municipal Court, Nita City, Nita.

1   floor. Detective Holmes of the Sheriff's Department was present and informed me that Holmes
2   had removed a knife from Mr. Baker's right hand. I noticed that there was a good deal of blood
3   in the palm area of his right hand. Detective Holmes informed me that the knife also had blood
4   on the handle in the area where the hand would grip the knife. Mr. Baker had very evidently
5   been shot. Inferior to the right scapula were elliptical wounds compatible with an entry and exit
6   gunshot wound. Upon turning his body over, an entry bullet wound was found on the right neck
7   slightly anterior to the angle of the mandible. A third entry wound was found in the upper right
8   chest wall, and a fourth entry wound was located at the anterior right shoulder.
9
10 I immediately questioned whether Mr. Baker was holding the knife when shot, since in my
11 professional experience, a person who is gripping a knife when shot and is still holding the knife
12 when he expires would normally not have blood on the palm or the knife handle, as the grip would
13 insulate both areas from blood.
14
15 While I was at Ashgate, I saw the defendant, who was being detained by Detective Holmes
16 and a sheriff's deputy. I looked at her left arm, which had some three to four superficial, shallow
17 scratches or knife cuts that were clustered and parallel to each other. They were consistent with
18 wounds that have been self-inflicted. None was life threatening in any way. They did not require
19 bandaging.
20
21 Deputy Coroner Beazley took custody of the body, placing it in a body bag, and we returned
22 with the body to the Coroner's Office. When we arrived, the body of Kelly Baker was placed in the
23 morgue. Later that day Detective Holmes, with my permission, took a full set of fingerprints and
24 Mr. Baker's robe and pajamas. At Holmes's request, I took a vial of blood from Mr. Baker's body,
25 sealed it, and gave it to Detective Holmes as evidence.
26
27 I performed a general autopsy examination on the body of Kelly Baker at the Darrow County
28 Coroner's Office on September 8, 2012, at approximately 8:30 a.m. Kelly Baker was thirty-four years
29 old, six feet in height, weighed 170 pounds, and had light brown hair and brown eyes. He showed
30 no external evidence of trauma other than the bullet wounds, which I will describe in detail.
31
32 I then performed an internal examination. I found no evidence of trauma, illness, or any other
33 factor that would contribute to the cause of death other than gunshot wounds of the neck and
34 thorax. Mr. Baker was shot four times. I will describe these wounds by referring to them as wounds
35 one, two, three, and four. Wound number one entered Mr. Baker's face on the right side eight
36 inches below the top of his head. The wound track led backward, downward, and leftward. The
37 bullet perforated the right carotid artery causing significant bleeding. I located a bullet that was
38 deformed from subcutaneous tissue in his back approximately ten inches below the top of his
39 head. I turned over possession of the recovered bullet to Detective Holmes early that afternoon.
40
41 Wound number two entered Mr. Baker's right upper chest right of the midline. The wound
42 track traveled backward, downward, and leftward, perforating both the right upper and lower
43 lung lobes, the pulmonary arteries, the left upper and lower lung lobes, and exited the back about
44 five inches lower than it entered and about a foot left of the entrance wound. This wound also
45 caused considerable bleeding.

1   Wound number three entered Mr. Baker's right shoulder about ten inches below the top of his
2   head and about seven inches to the right of the front midline. This wound track also traveled back-
3   ward, downward, and leftward and perforated the head of his humerus, which is the upper arm
4   bone. The wound track perforated the cervical vertebra number five, the left clavicle, and came
5   to a stop just in front of the head of the left humerus. I recovered a deformed bullet, which I later
6   turned over to Detective Holmes.

7

8   Wound number four entered Mr. Baker's right back about one-and-a-half feet below the top of
9   his head and about four inches to the right of the midline. This wound track traveled downward
10   and leftward, traversing to the right back where it exited at about the same distance from the top
11   of the head about two inches to the right of the midline.

12

13   I did not detect any powder debris at the site or in the wound track of any of the four wounds.
14   This would indicate that the shots were not fired from a close distance. Assuming that Mr. Baker
15   was attacking Mrs. Baker with a knife and was able to get close enough to inflict knife wounds to
16   her left arm, I would certainly expect to find powder debris on his body or clothing under such a
17   factual scenario.

18

19   In my opinion, death occurred sometime between 8:00 and 8:15 a.m. From the angle of the
20   wounds and the position of blood found at the scene, Mr. Baker was most likely seated when he
21   was shot.

Cross-Examination

1   There is no certification one can acquire to become an expert in gunshot wound deaths or
2   trajectory analysis. There are no specific courses given in medical school dealing specifically with
3   these areas. The position of the wound tracks leading from a higher to a lower position on the
4   body of Mr. Baker indicate that if Mr. Baker was in an upright position and the gun was fired by a
5   person standing, the body was in a lower position such as a seated position. However, if Mr. Baker
6   was standing in a semicrouch facing Mrs. Baker, then the wound tracks for wounds number one,
7   two, and three would be consistent with such a position. However, certainly wound number four is
8   not consistent with that scenario because the wound entered the back. Also, there was blood found
9   on the chair that was consistent with Mr. Baker's blood.

10

11   I did examine the G.I. tract and found contents in the stomach, but I cannot tell you whether
12   the contents were from a croissant or orange juice. I am not aware that any effort was made by law
13   enforcement to determine whether those contents were in Mrs. Baker's stomach that morning.

14

15   My practice has included studies in the field of the effects of alcohol on the human body and
16   mind, observing individuals in various stages of intoxication, correlating their behavior with blood
17   alcohol levels, and on occasion testifying in court concerning my findings and conclusions in indi-
18   vidual cases. I have been found by courts to be an expert in this field on at least five occasions. The
19   blood sample taken from Mr. Baker was found by analysis to contain .08 percent by weight. While
20   individuals vary as to their ability to function at different blood alcohol levels, in my opinion all
21   people would be appreciably impaired by alcohol at .08 percent sufficiently that they could not

1   safely operate a motor vehicle. Certainly all persons would have significant impairment of judg-
2   ment, of visual acuity, of physical coordination, and of general perception of events. It is also not
3   unusual for one who generally has an even disposition and temper to become combative and vio-
4   lent when under the influence of alcohol. I have seen this change in behavior in many individuals
5   and have read definitive studies in the field that substantiate this. I am familiar with the concepts
6   of absorption and dissipation or burn-off as they relate to alcohol ingestion. It is true that the
7   alcohol percentage in Mr. Baker's body does not tell us when he drank the alcohol. He could have
8   consumed the alcohol sometime shortly before the shooting or he could have consumed it several
9   hours before. If he had consumed it several hours before, he would have burned off alcohol at a
10   rate somewhere around .02 percent per hour. If he had his last drink the night before around mid-
11   night, his blood alcohol level could well have been in the neighborhood of .20 or higher around
12   1:00 a.m. It would certainly be possible for someone with a .20 blood alcohol level to have greatly
13   impaired judgment, and some people at that level are capable of harboring violent thoughts.
14

15   I do know of Dr. Leslie Torgeson. I am aware that Dr. Torgeson has made telephone inquiries
16   at our office about this case. Dr. Torgeson was a professional associate in the Darrow County
17   Coroner's Office for about three years and then moved to Marshall City. Dr. Torgeson apparently
18   was unhappy at not being promoted to director of the Coroner's Office Pathology Laboratory.
19   I have attended meetings of pathologists when Dr. Torgeson has been discussed. Dr. Torgeson has
20   apparently said that Dr. Torgeson knows more than any of the pathologists in Nita and should
21   have been made the director of the Laboratory. I have no idea what Dr. Torgeson's opinion is con-
22   cerning this case, as I have not discussed the case with Dr. Torgeson.

    I hereby certify that the foregoing is a true and correct transcription of the testimony of Dr. Morgan Sain on October 20, 2012, at the preliminary hearing in *State v. Baker,* in the Darrow County Municipal Court, Nita City, Nita.

Certified by:

Julian Lanfranconi

Julian Lanfranconi
Court Reporter

Testimony of Dale Ryan at Preliminary Hearing[3]

Direct Examination

1   I am a forensic scientist with the Bureau of Forensic Science in the Darrow County Sheriff's
2 Department. My duties include crime scene investigation and reconstruction, analysis of con-
3 trolled substances, examination and identification of body fluids, DNA analysis, firearms exami-
4 nation and identification, operation of the Integrated Ballistics Identification System, known as
5 IBIS, toolmark examination, shoe print and tire track examination, and where appropriate to give
6 expert testimony. Exhibit 1 is my professional resume and sets forth accurately and completely my
7 background and qualifications in these areas.
8

9   On September 7 of this year shortly after 1:00 p.m. I was notified by Detective Holmes of our
10 department that a homicide had occurred at Ashgate Farm. Detective Holmes had obtained a
11 search warrant, and we drove to Ashgate shortly before 2:00 p.m. We first went to the second level
12 and examined two bedrooms where Detective Holmes seized certain evidence. We then went to
13 the kitchen on the first floor. Detective Holmes pointed out to me where the body of Kelly Baker
14 was lying earlier and where the nine-mm Luger and casings were located. I then measured the
15 distances from the body to the chair, the table, the pistol, the casings, blood spatter on the east
16 wall, and the bullet holes in the east wall. I took swabs of blood spots on the floor, the chair, and
17 the spatter on the wall. I also retrieved from the east wall two bullets. I gave all items of evidence
18 to Detective Holmes for safekeeping after first placing each evidence item in a sealed container or
19 envelope and properly initialing each.
20

21   Shortly before 5:00 p.m. I went to the morgue and conducted a gunshot residue test on the
22 body of Kelly Baker. I found no traces of primer residue on any portion of his body.
23

24   The next day around 10:00 in the morning I went to our Bureau of Identification and picked up
25 twenty items of evidence that Detective Holmes had turned over to that office. They were marked
26 as Items 1 through 9 and 17 through 27. Later that day Detective Holmes delivered to me four-
27 teen more items of evidence marked Items 10 through 16 and 28 through 34. I then proceeded to
28 conduct a DNA analysis, a saliva detection analysis, a powder residue examination of Kelly Baker's
29 clothing, a firearms examination and identification analysis, and a scene reconstruction.
30

31   My DNA analysis involved looking at ten different evidence items, including blood samples
32 from both Kelly Baker and the defendant. I made comparisons between evidence items and the
33 known blood typing of both the defendant and Mr. Baker where I was able to isolate and amplify
34 results through DNA analysis.

---

[3] The transcript of Dale Ryan's testimony was excerpted so that only Dale Ryan's answers are reprinted here. Assume that this is a true and accurate rendering of Dale Ryan's answers. The testimony was given at the preliminary hearing on October 20, 2011, in the Darrow County Municipal Court, Nita City, Nita.

1   The knife, evidence Item 2, had blood stains on both sides of the blade at the tip and on the
2   handle. I was unable to conclusively type the blood on one side at the tip, but was able to deter-
3   mine that the blood on the other side at the tip was consistent with a mixture of the blood of both
4   Kelly Baker and the defendant. The blood on the knife's handle was consistent with Kelly Baker's
5   blood and inconsistent with that of the defendant. There was quite a bit of blood on the handle
6   and no blood on the blade except for the tip. My conclusion from these facts is that it is very
7   unlikely that the knife was used in an attack by Mr. Baker, as had such an attack occurred, there
8   would most likely have been blood drops and spatter on the blade from Mr. Baker's wounds, and
9   there would not have been much, if any, blood on the handle at the spot where he was supposed
10   to be holding the knife.
11
12   The DNA profile of blood consistent with the defendant's and inconsistent with Kelly Baker's
13   was found on the instep of the defendant's right shoe, stains on the interior of her blouse at the left
14   rear sleeve, the interior hem of the right rear side, and the right front sleeve and from the swab of
15   blood on the floor in front of the sink.
16
17   The DNA profile of blood consistent with Kelly Baker's and inconsistent with the defendant's,
18   in addition to that found on the knife handle, was found on the bottom of the defendant's right
19   shoe, the stains on the chair and the kitchen wall, on the exterior right rear arm seam of the defen-
20   dant's blouse, and all samples taken from Kelly Baker's robe and pajamas, which included the right
21   rear of the pants, both legs down the thighs, and on the center rear back. No other conclusive
22   DNA results were obtained. Because the blood spatter was consistent with Mr. Baker's blood,
23   I conducted a separate amylase mapping test to determine whether saliva was present. If saliva was
24   present, then the spatter could come from atomized droplets aspirated from Mr. Baker through
25   coughing or sneezing. The test did not reveal the presence of any saliva.
26
27   I examined Mr. Baker's robe and pajamas for evidence of powder residue and found none.
28   I then conducted a firearms examination and identification analysis. Evidence Item 1 was a nine-
29   mm Luger semiautomatic pistol in operating condition. It appeared to be a World War II model.
30   I conducted a firearms comparison test and determined that this pistol fired all four recovered bul-
31   lets, two from Kelly Baker's body and two from the wall. Also, the pistol fired the four cartridge
32   cases found at the scene. I compared the casings at the scene and the live rounds in the pistol's
33   magazine with the nine-mm ammunition recovered from the defendant's bedroom, and they were
34   the same type and brand. I test-fired Item 1 and found that gunpowder residue was left when fired
35   from muzzle to target at a distance of four feet or less. That led me to conclude that the muzzle of
36   the gun the defendant fired had to have been more than four feet from Kelly Baker's body at the
37   time of firing.
38
39   I then conducted an examination of Kelly Baker's pajamas and robe and found holes consistent
40   with his wounds to the right shoulder and right upper chest as well as one entrance and two exit
41   holes in the back, which are consistent with the right-to-left grazing wound and the separate exit
42   wound in his left back. I examined his robe and pajamas and did not find any gunshot residue.
43
44   When I reconstructed the shooting, I noted that the blood spatter, Item 15, was measured at
45   forty-two to forty-six inches from the floor. The spatter pattern was consistent with a medium to

1   high-velocity gunshot. The blood spotting was atomized and was less than one mm in diameter. It
2   was consistent with having been twenty to thirty inches from the wound of Mr. Baker. I prepared
3   Exhibit 2 from extensive testing, which illustrates the appearance of high-velocity blood spatter at
4   varying distances. You can see from the top of the exhibit that the spatter in this case ranged from
5   the first to the second box. This, of course, would suggest that Mr. Baker, when he was shot, was
6   no further from the wall than thirty or possibly forty inches and was consistent with his being in a
7   seated position when he suffered the wound. That is further supported by the amylase examination
8   eliminating aspiration as the cause of the spatter. The distance of the spatter from the wound also
9   indicates that Mr. Baker was not attacking the defendant, as she claimed, but rather was on the
10 east side of the kitchen at the table.
11
12 In my reconstruction, I used a Styrofoam dummy to establish the trajectory of the bullets using
13 the position of the blood spatter, the location of the wounds to Mr. Baker, the blood found on the
14 chair, and the position of the two recovered bullets in the east wall. The only reasonable conclusion
15 I could come to was that Mr. Baker was seated at a distance more than four feet from the defendant
16 when he was shot.

CROSS-EXAMINATION

1   Certainly I was not there at the time of the shooting, so I have to rely on my reconstruction
2   analysis for my opinion. It is true that forensic scientists do offer differing opinions in many cases
3   on matters of the kind involved in this case. I have not discussed this case with Dr. Torgeson and
4   therefore do not know what Dr. Torgeson's opinion is in this case. It is true that I have worked with
5   Dr. Torgeson in past years and found Dr. Torgeson's work to be professional and expert.
6
7   While I took measurements of two different positions of the blood spatter and determined
8   them to be forty and forty-six inches from the floor, I did not take measurements of any of the
9   other areas of the spatter. However, in looking at the spatter, it appeared to me to be all within
10 the range of forty to forty-six inches. I did not take measurements of the distance from the center
11 or the edges of the spatter to the north wall. It is true that I did not photograph the spatter, but
12 I have years of experience in such examinations and know that the appearance was as I indicated
13 on Exhibit 2. It is true that I did not measure each individual spatter to determine if it was one
14 mm or less.
15
16 The bloodstains on both legs of Mr. Baker's pajamas did extend down the front of his pants.
17 Such stains would be consistent with what are called "elongated bloodstains." There was so much
18 blood on the pajama legs that it would be hard to determine whether the spotting was round or
19 elongated. It is true that if the spotting was elongated, that could be consistent with Mr. Baker
20 losing the blood from the upper body wounds dropping onto his legs while he was in a standing
21 position. If Mr. Baker was standing when he was shot and then fell back in the area of the chair,
22 I would expect to find blood in the area of the chair where it was located.
23
24 I cannot tell you which shots were fired in what order. That is not possible. I did not detect
25 any bodily fluids or residue on the bullets recovered during the autopsy in this case in my DNA
26 analysis. I did not find any trace evidence on any bullet that could be matched with the clothing

1   that Mr. Baker was wearing. If Mr. Baker was approaching the defendant with a knife in his right

2   hand and he was in a crouched position with his body more than four feet from the muzzle of the

3   pistol and at a position slightly left of the defendant as he was facing her, this could be consistent

4   with the trajectory of the bullet paths through Mr. Baker's body. If Mr. Baker, after being shot,

5   turned and was shot in the back and then fell to the chair and then onto the floor, this would be

6   consistent with the position of the wounds and the blood found on the chair. If, before he fell, he

7   were to cough or sneeze, that could account for the spatter forty to forty-six inches from the floor

8   on the east wall. However, you would expect to find saliva present in such spatter, and you would

9   certainly expect to find Mr. Baker's blood on the knife blade. It is true that if Mr. Baker's grip on

10   the knife blade relaxed, then blood could conceivably invade the space between his right palm and

11   the knife handle.

12

13   In my examination of the blood sample taken from Mr. Baker's body, I did find that there was

14   .08 percent blood alcohol by weight. Such a level is consistent with one's having impaired percep-

15   tion, judgment, and motor skills. It is also true that some people at such a blood alcohol level

16   exhibit aggressive and violent tendencies not displayed when they are sober. When you ask me to

17   assume hypothetically that Mr. Baker in the past has displayed such violent tendencies after he has

18   been drinking, then I would agree that it would not be unusual for him to display such tendencies

19   on other occasions.

I hereby certify that the foregoing is a true and correct transcription of the testimony of Dale Ryan on October 20, 2012, at the preliminary hearing in *State v. Baker*, in the Darrow County Municipal Court, Nita City, Nita.

Certified by:

Julian Lanfranconi

Julian Lanfranconi
Court Reporter

Exhibit 1

RESUME OF DALE R. RYAN
FORENSIC SCIENTIST

EDUCATION

B.S. Forensic Science with distinction, May 2000, Nita State University. Minor in Chemistry.
M.S. Forensic Science, June 2002, Nita University.

EMPLOYMENT HISTORY

Forensic Scientist III, Darrow County Sheriff's Department, April 2009 to present.
Forensic Scientist II, Darrow County Sheriff's Department, April 2007 to April 2009.
Criminalist II, District Attorney's Laboratory of Criminalistics, Sheldon County, Nita, July 2005 to April 2007.
Criminalist I, Arizona Department of Public Safety, Eastern Regional Crime Laboratory, Mesa, Arizona, September 2001 to July 2005.
Fellowship, FBI Laboratory, Washington, D.C. Special studies in serology and DNA testing, June 2002 to August 2003.

PROFESSIONAL MEMBERSHIPS

International Association of Blood Pattern Analysts since 2011.
International Association for Identification since 2007.
Nita Association of Crime Scene Investigators since 2007.
Association of Firearm and Toolmark Examiners since 2006 (Distinguished Member status).
American Academy of Forensic Sciences since 2009.

CERTIFICATION

Nita Association of Forensic Scientists, 2007.
Diplomate, American Board of Criminalistics, 2010 to present.

SPECIAL TRAINING

Crime Scene Investigation and Reconstruction—Over 160 hours including specialized courses in Bloodstain Evidence, Gunshot Trajectory, and Blood Spatter Documentation.
Firearms Related—More than 180 hours including specialized courses in Firearm and Toolmark Identification, Forensic Wound Pathology, and Wound Ballistics.
Trace Evidence and Serology Related—Over 250 hours including specialized training in DNA Analysis and Typing Methods, Hair/Fiber and Blood Collection and Analysis, Semen and Saliva Analysis, Human Population Genetics, Applied Molecular Spectroscopy, and Advanced Forensic Microscopy.

PROFESSIONAL PUBLICATIONS

Reconstruction of Gunshot Homicide with Claim of Self-Defense, *American Forensic Science Quarterly*, October 2007.
Firearms Comparison with Remington Brand Caliber .22 Rimfire Bullets, *Police Science Journal*, February 2005.
Shooting Reconstructions Utilizing Blood Spatter Patterns, *Nita Criminalistics Journal*, November 2009.
Preparation for a *Kelly* Admissibility Hearing in a RFLP DNA Case, *National Institute of Justice Review*, December 2011.

TEACHING EXPERIENCE

Adjunct Professor at Nita State University, January 2011 to present. Teach Biological Evidence Examination.

Guest Lecturer at Nita State University, Nita University, Arizona State University, and the FBI Academy. Lectured on DNA Typing Methods, Crime Scene Investigation and Reconstruction, Gunshot Trajectory, and Firearms Examination and Identification.

Staff and Guest Instructor for Law Enforcement Training Programs including courses presented by the Darrow County Sheriff's Department, the Nita City Police Department, the Nita State Investigators Association, and the Nita Crime Scene Investigators Association.

Exhibit 2

HIGH-VELOCITY SPATTERING—SIZE AND PROJECTED DISTANCE

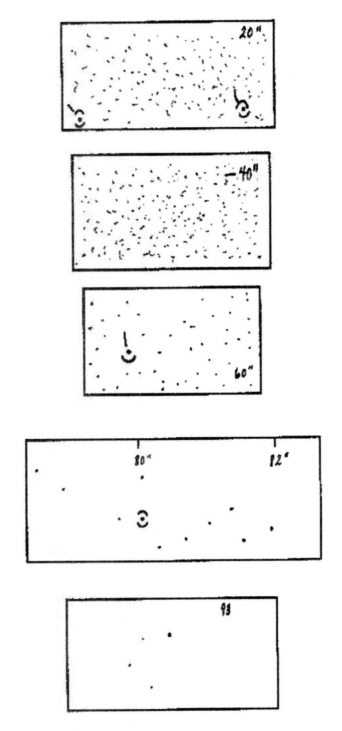

Testimony of Kit Manville at Preliminary Hearing[4]

Direct Examination

1   I live at 19925 Talbot Road in Darrow County about ten miles north of Warrenton. I am a far-
2   rier and a musician and singer. For about two and a half years I worked for Sarah Baker at Ashgate
3   Farm. Then Ms. Baker fired me because she was afraid I knew too much about her cheating on
4   her husband.
5

6   For about the first year I was very happy at Ashgate. Everyone treated me well, and I was con-
7   stantly praised by the Bakers and by the manager, Chris Spahn. I made several recommendations
8   that changed the system of shoeing the horses and caring for them. Also, I was constantly asked to
9   entertain at the Ashgate parties. I played the guitar and sang folk and bluegrass songs. Mr. Baker
10   told me that I was the best thing that happened to their polo pony raising program.
11

12   I did witness Ms. Baker in a pretty violent incident about a year and a half ago. After that inci-
13   dent, Ms. Baker's attitude toward me changed. The whole thing stemmed over a customer, Will
14   White, who was upset because his pony died shortly after he bought it from Ashgate. He came
15   to Ashgate about seven in the evening. I was still working, and he stopped and asked me where
16   Ms. Baker was. I could tell that he was perturbed, so after I told him where the Ashgate residence
17   was, I walked over there to make sure things were OK. I saw White go to the door and then
18   Ms. Baker walked out. She started shouting right away. She told him to get off the property. He
19   walked away and said something about suing her. She ran in the house and came out with a gun.
20   I could see her pointing the gun in his direction, and then I heard a loud bang. I thought maybe
21   she had shot him, but then I saw Mr. White run away. I remember her saying something like,
22   "Next time you come here you're going to be carried out."
23

24   She then walked back in the house. About five minutes later she walked out and headed down to
25   where I was finishing my work. I saw her coming and walked out to meet her. She said, "You know,
26   Kit, we at Ashgate have to stick together. That's part of being part of the Ashgate family. You know
27   that man was going to attack me. I had to defend myself. My daddy a long time ago showed me
28   how to protect myself. That's why I have what he calls 'the equalizer,' a nine-mm equalizer." I just
29   nodded. She said that I should talk to Chris Spahn, and Chris would explain how to deal with
30   the Sheriff's Office if there were any questions. She walked off. A little later the sheriff's deputies
31   arrived and talked to me. I wasn't sure what to do, but I told them that White was really angry and
32   maybe Ms. Baker thought she needed to protect herself.

---

[4] The transcript of Kit Manville's testimony was excerpted so that only Kit Manville's answers are reprinted here. Assume that this is a true and accurate rendering of Kit Manville's answers. The testimony was given at the preliminary hearing on October 20, 2012, in the Darrow County Municipal Court, Nita City, Nita.

1   I guess Ms. Baker thought that I told the Sheriff's Office everything, because after that she
2   wouldn't talk to me. Her attorney talked to me once, and I told her the same thing. I don't know
3   exactly what happened with her case, but I understand she got some kind of a fine.
4

5   Shortly after that, Chris Spahn called me into the manager's office and told me that I was
6   being disciplined for drinking on the job and that my employment record would show that.
7   I told Chris that I did not drink on the job, and the only time that I had alcoholic drinks at
8   Ashgate was either when I was entertaining at their parties or when Mr. Baker would invite me
9   to have a drink. Actually, Mr. Baker and I did this pretty often. We got to be pretty good friends.
10   I think he felt left out, because it didn't appear to me that Ms. Baker paid much attention to him
11   that last year. In fact, Mr. Baker would ask me over drinks what was happening on the farm, and
12   I would give him the latest. I thought he ought to know that Ms. Baker was playing around on
13   him. She was spending a lot of time with this good-looking guy. I guess he was a DA. He was
14   always with her at Ashgate. She sure gave him looks she didn't give her husband, if you know
15   what I mean.
16

17   The first time I saw the two together was at the Community Games. Usually Ms. Baker and
18   Mr. Baker would be in the family box seats. This time Mr. Baker wasn't there, and she was with
19   the DA. I think it raised a few eyebrows, but after the games, a lot of the people who came to the
20   games went over to The Saddle, a fancy restaurant in Warrenton. I was there with some friends,
21   and I saw Ms. Baker and this fellow sitting by themselves in a corner booth. I watched them pretty
22   closely, because she was acting funny. She kept touching him. She would put her hand on his arm
23   while she was talking to him, and she looked at him the whole time. She never acted that way with
24   Mr. Baker.
25

26   I think the worst time was about two months ago when I saw Ms. Baker and this guy get out
27   of her fancy Lexus. I was down the road at the barn, but I could see them and hear them. They
28   both looked around, as if to see if anyone was there, and then they walked toward the house. She
29   had her head on his shoulder. I could hear her saying something like, "I just love the way you
30   are, Brad." He squeezed her shoulder, and they walked into the house. I could hear her laughing.
31   I knew something was up. Maybe an hour later they came out. I was still in the shop, maybe
32   100 feet away, and I could see that they had been up to something, because her hair was really
33   messed up. They got into the Lexus and drove off. I could see that she was putting lipstick on as
34   they drove away.
35

36   It was getting to the point where they were making a sucker out of poor Mr. Baker. The last straw
37   was about a week later when I heard Ms. Baker and Chris Spahn talking next door. Ms. Baker was
38   telling Chris something about cutting Mr. Baker out of the will. I believe the words she used were,
39   "I've decided Kelly is out of the will. Don't worry, I am still leaving your house to you. If Kelly gives
40   me any trouble, I know how to take care of him."
41

42   I waited until the next day, and then I called Mr. Baker and told him what I had heard. He
43   seemed very surprised but then said something like, "It's OK, Kit, I could see this coming. You are

1 a true friend. Don't worry, I won't forget it." He then told me that he was not going to give her a
2 divorce unless she gave him his fair share of the property. He said she would have to take him to
3 court, and he had talked to a lawyer, and the lawyer had said that they had a case and it would cost
4 Ms. Baker "millions." He said he was going to tell her that. I think that was the last time I ever
5 talked to Mr. Baker.
6
7   In just a matter of a few days Chris Spahn fired me and said that Ms. Baker was giving me three
8 months' severance pay even though I wasn't entitled to it. I demanded to know why I was being
9 fired, and Spahn told me that I had a real alcohol problem and it was affecting my work. That was
10 a big lie. The whole thing was a cover-up to get me out.

CROSS-EXAMINATION

1   It's true that Mr. Baker was upset at what was happening with this DA. Every time I told him
2 about one of those incidents, he would get really upset and would have several more drinks. I tried
3 to make him feel better by telling him that he was a nice guy and was really getting a raw deal.
4 I was never in the house when Ms. Baker and the guy named Brad were there. I couldn't say from
5 directly seeing them that they were engaged in romantic conduct. I know that I heard her say the
6 word "love," but I can't be sure that it wasn't something like, "I love the things you say" or "I love
7 the things you do." I can't remember whether they had papers they were carrying when they went
8 in the door.
9
10   I called Kelly Baker and told him that I had seen Ms. Baker and this fellow Brad at The Saddle
11 Restaurant. I thought he ought to know. I have no idea whether Ms. Baker had already told
12 Mr. Baker about inviting Brad to the Community Games or whether she told him about the
13 restaurant.
14
15   It is true that the first part of this year I was sentenced to ninety days in jail for a new DUI and
16 for violation of probation, and Ms. Baker did agree with the Probation Department to set up a
17 work furlough arrangement so I could work during the ninety days and I would do the jail time in
18 the evening. I guess if I had to do the straight ninety days in jail she could have fired me because
19 I wasn't available to work. I realize that I have had a drinking problem that led to three DUI con-
20 victions, but I have kept my drinking separate from my work.
21
22   I had a little problem about six years ago when I was working for Barrett Farms. I was in charge
23 of the stables. An owner had left a horse there for boarding and grooming. She was going to be
24 out of the country for several weeks, and I thought it was a shame that this horse wasn't being rid-
25 den, so I loaned it out to a customer. I charged the customer $500 to use the horse for the week.
26 I kept $200 of that for my fee. I guess what happened was the owner came back and somehow
27 found out that her horse had been loaned out. She was pretty mad and reported it to the Sheriff's
28 Department. I pled guilty and paid a fine. In looking back, it was a stupid thing to do, but it
29 didn't seem to me at the time to be bad because the horse would get exercise and my employer and
30 I would make a little money.

I hereby certify that the foregoing is a true and correct transcription of the testimony of Kit Manville on October 20, 2012, at the preliminary hearing in *State v. Baker,* in the Darrow County Municipal Court, Nita City, Nita.

Certified by:

Julian Lanfranconi

Julian Lanfranconi
Court Reporter

STATEMENT OF CHRIS SPAHN[5]

1   I live at 8718 Springs Road in Warrenton, directly down the road from the Ashgate residence at
2   Ashgate Farm. I am the manager of Ashgate Farm. I have worked for Sarah Baker since 2006, and
3   I knew her for at least three years before I became the manager. I graduated from Nita University
4   in 2003 with a degree in Business. My family has been interested in polo for decades, and as a
5   child I rode horses and watched my father play polo and my brother play polo. After graduating,
6   I worked for Thompson Farms as an assistant manager, and in 2006 Sarah Baker offered me the job
7   of manager of Ashgate. My duties include direct responsibility for overseeing the entire operations,
8   including the renting of facilities for polo, raising polo ponies, and providing polo and horse rid-
9   ing lessons. Ashgate Farm employs approximately thirty employees, fifteen of whom are full-time.
10
11   Sarah Baker is one of the most gentle and caring people I know. She is scrupulously honest and
12   very loyal and supportive to her employees. I could not have a better employer, and I consider her
13   a true friend.
14
15   About five years ago Sarah met Kelly Baker and was very impressed with him. They began to see
16   a lot of each other, and often he came to the farm. Initially I liked him. He was personable, and he
17   seemed to care very much for Sarah. However, he was at a party following a match one night when
18   he had too much to drink, and he really got nasty. He uttered a few obscenities and refused to go
19   home with Sarah. It was so embarrassing that most everyone left. I think that was shortly after they
20   were married. After Sarah and Mr. Baker were married, I began to notice a change in their relation-
21   ship. During the year before their marriage they were always happy together. But gradually after
22   their marriage they became more distant. Mr. Baker seemed to be gone most of the time. I really
23   didn't see him that often, and when I did, he usually didn't stop to talk to me. He just ignored me.
24   I began to worry about Sarah. She's very sensitive, and I knew that this must be bothering her, but
25   I wasn't going to say anything unless she talked to me. Sarah and I worked very closely together,
26   so I had plenty of opportunities to see the change in her. Lately she has seemed lonely and sad.
27
28   About a week before the shooting I remember that Sarah was especially sad. In fact, she looked
29   like she had been crying. I asked her if she was all right, and she said that she was sad because one
30   of her family treasures, a china lamp, had been broken and couldn't be replaced. I said something
31   like, "Maybe you can find another like it." She said, "No" and just shook her head.
32
33   The times that Sarah seemed most happy in the last year were when she was working on Project
34   WEB. She told me several times that she was blessed with a fortune, and she had a responsibility to
35   help others less fortunate. She thought that Project WEB was one way to do that. Sarah for years
36   has been holding charity events at Ashgate, and now she saw an opportunity to do that and tie it in
37   with a community effort to build a home and center for abused women. She worked with a num-
38   ber of people including county officials. One was a very nice young man named Brad McCormick.
39   He seemed very interested in helping, and he was at Ashgate a number of times helping to plan

---

[5] This statement was given to defense investigator Baxter Franklin in his office on October 14, 2012.

1   events. I think Sarah was her happiest in the last year when the two of them were making progress
2   on the center. She talked about that quite often. It wasn't anything romantic. They just shared a
3   very strong common interest in Project WEB.
4
5   The first time I saw anything really wrong with Sarah and Mr. Baker was the night before the
6   shooting. Sarah and I were going over some business matters at her home. We had just finished
7   about 7:00 p.m. and were talking on the front porch. Mr. Baker drove up, parked his car directly
8   in front of the porch, and walked over. He gave me a dirty look and then looked at Sarah and said
9   something about the will. He was really mad. Sarah seemed embarrassed and looked over at me.
10 Mr. Baker didn't look at me and spoke to Sarah, telling her he wanted an answer. I left as quickly
11 as I could. I was worried about Sarah, but I didn't think it was my place to interfere.
12
13 The next morning I was in the business office, which is at the front of my home. I got a call from
14 Sarah at 8:30 a.m. I know the time because I had a telephone appointment at 8:15, and I had just
15 completed the call. Sarah was crying. She said that something terrible had happened and asked
16 that I come immediately. I ran to her house. Sarah was on the porch with her two hands over her
17 face crying. She had blood on her arm, and I could see several cuts still bleeding. I asked her what
18 happened. Sarah said Mr. Baker went crazy and told her that he was going to kill her. She said that
19 Mr. Baker pointed a gun at her, and she was able to convince him to put it down. Then he got a
20 kitchen knife and tried to slash her. We walked in the house and Sarah said, "I had to do it. He
21 would have killed me." I saw Mr. Baker lying on the floor. He was holding a knife. He looked like
22 he was dead. The kitchen was a bloody mess. The gun was lying on the floor. Sarah then said that
23 they had to call 911 and went over to the phone and called. Soon the sheriffs arrived.
24
25 I am not surprised that Mr. Baker was angry. If he was anything like he was the night before,
26 then he was out of control. Poor Sarah. This whole experience has been horrible for her. First, she
27 was nearly killed, and if she hadn't defended herself, she would have been. Now she has been falsely
28 accused of murder. Fortunately, Mr. McCormick has been calling her and supporting her. Sarah
29 has said several times that she didn't know how she would get through this without Brad's help.
30 About a year after I came to work at Ashgate, one of the employees, a clerk, claimed I was altering
31 the books and pocketing money. She was disgruntled because she had not been promoted, and she
32 didn't like me from the day I arrived. I was arrested by the Sheriff's Office. I explained the whole
33 thing to Sarah, and she immediately went down to the Sheriff's Office and told them that it was a
34 big mistake. They dropped the charges. Obviously, the clerk had to be discharged for making false
35 accusations. The clerk later filed suit for wrongful discharge, and it was settled for nuisance value
36 of $10,000.
37
38 Four years ago this month I was falsely accused of diverting employment benefits. The whole
39 matter was simply a big mistake. Two employees claimed that I had not been submitting dis-
40 ability benefit taxes for them, and they were not eligible for disability. There was some confusion
41 as to whether they were eligible, but my attorney recommended that I plead guilty in exchange
42 for straight probation and a fine. I took the attorney's advice and pled, but in thinking about it,
43 I probably should have fought it, because I never intended to use any of the money for myself, even
44 though the two employees accused me of doing that. They were both friends of the clerk that had
45 me arrested two years before.

I have read the above statement consisting of two pages, and it is true and correct.

Signed: *Chris Spahn*   Date: October 14, 2012

Chris Spahn

Witnessed: *Baxter Franklin*   Date: October 14, 2012

Baxter Franklin

Statement of Bradley McCormick[6]

1   I am the chief deputy district attorney for Darrow County. I have been a prosecuting attorney
2   for nine years and the chief deputy for the last three years. My career as a prosecuting attorney is
3   very important to me. For as long as I can remember, I have wanted to be a DA. I grew up in a
4   poor neighborhood in Nita City. I remember feeling the hopelessness of the poor, and I remem-
5   ber seeing my poor mother beaten by my drunken father. It left a lasting impression on me. As a
6   prosecuting attorney, I had an opportunity to do something for all the people of our community,
7   including the poor people. The present district attorney, Ellen Forrest, has announced her plans to
8   run for the State Senate, and I have been urged to run for the district attorney in two years. I live
9   in Nita City and am single. I was divorced from my first wife two years ago.
10
11   Sarah Baker and I are professional colleagues in the sense that we have worked together on com-
12   munity projects. I want to stress very strongly that while we are certainly good friends, there is
13   absolutely no romantic relationship at all. I believe very strongly in what Sarah is trying to do for
14   battered women, and I have worked very hard to help her. It is true that we have many common
15   interests. I have a very keen interest in polo. I learned to play polo when I got a scholarship to a
16   prep school, St. Michael's Academy. Then when I got a scholarship to Stanford, I joined the polo
17   team. After college and law school I played as an amateur for The Grounders, one of the estab-
18   lished polo teams in Darrow County.
19
20   I first met Sarah at a meeting of the Darrow County Battered Women Council about a year ago.
21   County officials and community leaders were present. Sarah was introduced to me as the director
22   of Project WEB. I knew who she was and knew of her interest in polo, and I knew that she held
23   charity events at Ashgate. I suggested to her that funding for a battered women center could be
24   developed through events at Ashgate. She liked the idea and told me that the Community Games
25   were being held in a couple of months and asked for my help on the council in getting approval
26   for directing some of the funds to the proposed Project WEB Center. I agreed. Later the council
27   approved the plan.
28
29   Sarah invited me to attend the games as a guest, and after the games, we talked about our
30   plans for the center. Sarah suggested that we finish our discussion over dinner at The Saddle, an
31   upscale restaurant in Warrenton. A number of the people who attended the games were present.
32   Apparently someone reported back to Kelly Baker about seeing us at the restaurant. I later got a
33   call from Sarah informing me that Kelly was upset and accused her of "trolling for playmates."
34   I told her that I would be happy to talk with Kelly and explain, but she said not to worry, she
35   would take care of it. The next time I talked with Sarah about two weeks later she said there was no
36   problem with Kelly as she had taken care of it. For that reason, I did not worry about continuing
37   to meet Sarah at Ashgate.

---

[6] This statement was given to defense investigator Baxter Franklin in his office on October 14, 2012.

1   We met several more times at Ashgate. The passage you read me from Detective Holmes's state-
2   ment of someone named Manville is not correct. That's not the way it happened. It was about
3   three week ago. Sarah picked me up at my office, as we had to go over plans she had developed
4   for the center, and the plans were at Ashgate. We were there for only about one hour, and it was
5   all business. I don't remember talking outside the house, although we could have, but I know that
6   Sarah's hair was not messed. She is fastidious, and I have never seen her when she wasn't neat and
7   well groomed.
8
9   I explained to Detective Holmes that my note to Sarah was just an effort to encourage her to
10 keep her spirits up and continue her good work in Project WEB. I repeat, I have never engaged in
11 any intimate conduct with Sarah. I have great admiration for her, and I would happily serve as a
12 character witness for her in any upcoming trial. I do not believe for a moment that she would ever
13 commit murder. If she fired the gun that killed Kelly Baker, then I believe she did it only to protect
14 herself. It is true that I have continued to offer my support to Sarah by calling her. I believe that
15 anyone who felt the way I do about Sarah would do the same.

I have read the above statement consisting of two pages, and it is true and correct.

Signed: *Bradley McCormick*   Date: October 14, 2012
Bradley McCormick

Witnessed: *Baxter Franklin*   Date: October 14, 2012
Baxter Franklin

October 18, 2012

Clifford Berres, Esq.
Masi Berres & Shoun
868 Stock Drive
Nita City, Nita 55058

Dear Mr. Berres:

Thank you for your referral of Ms. Baker's case. As you requested, I have reviewed the case materials that you submitted, and I have enclosed a copy of my curriculum vitae. Those materials are the sheriff's reports prepared by Detective Holmes and Robin Mulligan, the police reports concerning Kelly Baker, the report of Forensic Scientist Dale Ryan and autopsy report prepared by Dr. Morgan Sain, copies of the two letters and the note recovered in this case, copies of the photos and diagrams, and copies of the two reports by Baxter Franklin.

Position of Kelly Baker When Shot

After careful review of the autopsy protocol by Dr. Morgan Sain, no major inconsistencies are found that would in any way preclude the possibility, if not probability, that the decedent Kelly Baker was advancing toward Ms. Baker and attacking her when the shots were fired. Only in a rare case is there definite anatomic evidence to support the position of the body in relation to a specific injury given the number of variables that must be taken into consideration. For example, without knowing the order of the gunshot wounds and whether the decedent Kelly Baker was trying to "twist" out of the way, no definite opinions can be made as to the exact location of the body in relation to the weapon.

Gunshot wound number four is of special interest. This wound, which is a grazing injury, is best depicted in the diagram and shows the entrance and exit wound to be at the same level, that is to say, horizontally oriented. If the decedent was in a sitting position as the prosecution contends, then the weapon, if Ms. Baker was standing, had to be fired with the weapon held at waist level (firing from the hip). This would be a most awkward position to shoot a firearm and very inaccurate. Given that Ms. Baker is the daughter of an international arms dealer, I would assume that she would know how to fire a weapon. Also, the trajectories of the remaining projectiles are from the side of the body, traveling from right to left. Again, if the decedent was sitting, as the prosecution contends, it would be more plausible for the wounds to travel in a more direct fashion from front to back.

The reason that no blood was found on the table was that Mr. Baker was not next to the table at the time he was shot. The blood spatter found was as consistent with the forceful expectoration of blood from the mouth as from a high-velocity occurrence. Mr. Baker could have attacked with a knife, been shot, twisted his body, and then been shot in the back, and then he fell in the area of the chair. That would explain the blood on the chair but not on the table. There is evidence that

Mr. Baker was standing upright during some of the blood loss. This produced elongated bloodstains down the front of his pajamas on both legs, consistent with a standing position.

Dale Ryan has concluded through a trajectory analysis that Mr. Baker was seated. Dale Ryan did not take sufficient measurements to make a positive trajectory conclusion. An alternative explanation of the observed facts would be that Mr. Baker was standing but crouched; that would result in a blood spatter that would be measured at forty-two to forty-six inches from the floor and would result in the bullets striking the east wall from thirty-one to thirty-three inches. Other alternatives can also be supported, including that Mr. Baker fell to his knees after receiving an initial bullet wound. It is my opinion, within a reasonable degree of medical certainty, that Mr. Baker's injuries are more consistent with his standing, presenting his right side to Ms. Baker, with his upper torso bent slightly forward, consistent with his using his right upper extremity to wield a weapon.

Sarah Baker's Wounds

I have reviewed Dr. Sain's autopsy report concerning Sarah Baker's wounds, and I am not aware of any scientific basis or literature that would confirm or deny Dr. Sain's supposition that the wounds on Sarah Baker were self-inflicted. I know of no way to prove one way or the other that the wounds were self-inflicted or caused by another; all that can be said is that they are consistent with incised, superficial wounds.

Presence of Blood on Kelly Baker's Right Hand and the Knife

In my experience as a forensic pathologist, I have personally reviewed cases where the deceased was holding a knife and suffered fatal injuries. I have seen cases where the hand and the knife were blood-free and other cases where the hand and knife had the decedent's blood on both. There are a number of factors that could affect the outcome, including the tension with which the knife was held at death. It is clearly possible that the grip of the decedent relaxed prior to death, allowing blood from his body to infiltrate the palmar surface of the hand and the knife's handle.

Conclusion

While it is impossible from my review of the case to say that any or all of the facts positively prove any one factual scenario in this case, I can say that there is a reasonable possibility that Sarah Baker fired the pistol in an effort to protect herself from a knife attack by Kelly Baker, a possibility at least as reasonable as the theory that Kelly Baker was in a seated position.

Additional Background Information

There are a few areas that need amplification. I have examined hundreds of bodies at death scenes of all kinds as well as a number of homicide scenes after the body was transported. I have performed over 2,000 medicolegal autopsies and have supervised another 100–150. At least 35 percent of those cases involved gunshot wounds. I have qualified and testified as an expert witness in the states of Nita and California and in federal courts over 100 times. I have appeared in criminal proceedings for both the prosecution and defense and have been retained by plaintiff's and defense attorneys in civil matters. The areas of my testimony have included cause of death, natural disease, and the nature and causation of various injuries present in both deceased and surviving persons, including gunshot and knife wounds and crime scene reconstruction. I have rendered an expert opinion in court concerning gunshot wounds in approximately forty-five cases. I have also been involved in interpreting results of serology and toxicology testing. Northern Nita Forensic Pathology Laboratories provides forensic pathology services for Marshall County. I currently perform thirty to forty autopsies per month. I have additionally consulted for private attorneys, public defenders, and district attorneys in several dozen cases.

If I testify as an expert in this case, you should know that Dr. Morgan Sain and I once worked together in the Darrow County Coroner's Office. When Dr. Sain was appointed medical director of that office, I chose to leave and come to Marshall City with Northern Nita Forensic Pathology Laboratories. While I respect Dr. Sain's medical qualifications and ability, I found it difficult, as a number of other medical associates did, to work with Dr. Sain. Since then I have testified on a number of occasions in opposition to the conclusions of Dr. Sain. Unfortunately, Dr. Sain has not accepted well my contrary opinions and has attempted to bring into question my objectivity, competence, and ethics by filing a complaint with the American Board of Pathology. Dr. Sain contended in the complaint that I had altered a tissue specimen in an alleged jail suicide case where I had concluded that the inmate had been beaten by others, possibly jail personnel, before a rope was placed around his neck. Although the matter is pending, I have no doubt that the board will find the complaint groundless, as I have positive proof of the condition of the tissue specimen when I inspected it, because I photographed the specimen before concluding my examination. I don't believe Dr. Sain is aware of this proof.

To date I have devoted eight hours in case review, analysis, and the preparation of this report at the standard rate of $350 per hour for a total of $2,800. Professional time devoted to preparing for and attending court will be billed at the same rate. If you require additional information or would like to discuss the case further, please feel free to call me.

Sincerely,

Leslie Torgeson

Leslie Torgeson, MD

CURRICULUM VITAE
LESLIE TORGESON, MD

1601 Heffernan Drive, Suite 410
Marshall City, Nita 99915
(721) 555-6066
(721) 555-6067 (Fax)
ltorgeson@cray.nita. (E-mail)

EDUCATIONAL BACKGROUND

BS, with great distinction in Biology and Chemistry, Charleston Southern University, 1997
MD, fourth in class, Medical University of South Carolina, 2001
Residency in Anatomical and Clinical Pathology, University of California–Davis, 2001 to 2005

EMPLOYMENT HISTORY

Forensic Pathologist, Los Angeles Coroner's Office, 2005 to 2008
Forensic Pathologist, Darrow County Coroner's Office, 2008 to 2010
Assistant Medical Director, Darrow County Coroner's Office, 2010 to 2011
Forensic Pathologist, Northern Nita Forensic Pathology Laboratories, 2011 to present

CERTIFICATION AND LICENSURE

Diplomate, National Board of Medical Examiners—July 2002
California Physician's and Surgeon's License—July 2002
American Board of Pathology—Anatomic/Clinical Pathology—November 2005
American Board of Pathology—Forensic Pathology—May 2007
Nita Physician's and Surgeon's License—June 2008
American Board of Forensic Examiners—September 2012

TEACHING EXPERIENCE

Assistant and Associate Professor of Pathology, Nita University, 2008 to present
Guest lecturer, University of California–Davis, Darrow Community College, Glenback College

PRESENTATIONS

University of California–Davis—"Gunshot Wounds: Self-Defense or Murder?" May 2008.
Nita State Hospital—Fifth Annual Pathology Forum—"Forensic Aspects of Homicide," November 2008.
Marshall County Sheriff-Coroner's Death Investigation Course—"Introduction to Forensic Medicine," April 21, 2012.

PUBLICATIONS

Torgeson, L., Securing Evidence in Gunshot Wound Deaths, *Journal of Forensic Sciences*, May 2011.

Fernandez, D.E., and Torgeson, L., Examination of Toxicological Evidence in Homicides, *Journal of Police Science*, October 2010.

Scheffing, L., Objectivity vs. Advocacy, *Journal on Advocacy*, February 2010.

COMMITTEE APPOINTMENTS

LOS ANGELES COUNTY GUNSHOT DEATH REVIEW TEAM, 2007–2008. Multidisciplinary review team charged with analyzing gunshot wound deaths and recommending investigative and teaching improvements in such cases.

NITA SIDS PROTOCOL COMMITTEE, CONSULTANT, April 2009 to 2011. Committee responsible for producing final form of a sudden infant death autopsy protocol for Nita Department of Health, as mandated by Nita SB 1069.

MARSHALL COUNTY TOXICOLOGY REVIEW TEAM, August 2011 to present. Team formed as a pilot program sponsored by the state of Nita to investigate causes and recommend preventive strategies to mortality as a result of toxic substances.

NORTHERN NITA REGIONAL TRAUMA QUALITY IMPROVEMENT COMMITTEE, July 2011 to present. Acts to review quality assurance for trauma care in Northern Nita counties.

APPLICABLE NITA CRIMINAL CODE AND EMPLOYMENT CODE SECTIONS

SECTION 100 N.C.C. HOMICIDE, DEFINITION OF TERMS

1. Homicide means the killing of a person by another.

2. Person, when referring to the victim of a homicide, means a human being who had been born and was alive at the time of the homicidal act.

3. The term "after deliberation" means not only intentionally, but also that the decision to commit the act has been made after the exercise of reflection and judgment concerning the act. An act committed after deliberation is never one that has been committed in a hasty or impulsive manner.

SECTION 101 N.C.C. FIRST-DEGREE MURDER

1. A person commits the crime of first-degree murder if, after deliberation and with the intent to cause the death of a person other than himself or herself, he or she causes the death of that person or of another person.

2. If the first-degree murder was carried out for financial gain, or if the victim was a police officer, prosecutor, or judge, or if the murder was committed by means of a bomb, or if the defendant in this proceeding has been convicted of more than one offense of murder in the first degree, then the punishment shall be life without the possibility of parole.

3. All other first-degree murder shall be punishable by confinement in prison for twenty-five years to life.

SECTION 102 N.C.C. SECOND-DEGREE MURDER

1. A person commits the crime of second-degree murder if:

    a. He or she intentionally, but not after deliberation, causes the death of a person, or

    b. With intent to cause serious bodily injury to a person other than himself or herself, he or she causes the death of that person or of another person.

2. Second-degree murder is punishable by confinement in prison for fifteen years to life.

SECTION 103 N.C.C. VOLUNTARY MANSLAUGHTER

1. A person commits the crime of voluntary manslaughter when he or she intentionally, but not after deliberation, causes the death of a person upon a sudden quarrel or heat of passion.

2. Voluntary manslaughter is punishable by confinement in prison for five to fifteen years.

SECTION 104 N.C.C. CRIMINALLY NEGLIGENT HOMICIDE

1. A person commits the crime of criminally negligent homicide if:

   a. By conduct amounting to criminal negligence, he or she causes the death of a person, or

   b. He or she intentionally causes the death of a person but believes in good faith that circumstances exist that would justify the killing, but the belief that such circumstances exist is unreasonable.

2. A person acts with criminal negligence when, through a gross deviation from the standard of care that a reasonable person would exercise, he or she fails to perceive a substantial and unjustifiable risk that a result will occur or that a circumstance exists.

3. Criminally negligent homicide is a misdemeanor punishable by confinement in the county jail for up to one year, or by a fine of up to $10,000, or both.

SECTION 242 N.C.C. BATTERY

1. Every person who commits a battery is guilty of a misdemeanor.

2. A battery is any willful and unlawful use of force or violence upon the person of another.

3. A battery is punishable by confinement in the county jail for up to six months, or by a fine of up to $2,000, or both.

SECTION 490 N.C.C. PUNISHMENT FOR THEFT

1. Every person who is guilty of the theft of property of a value exceeding $400 is guilty of a felony punishable by confinement in prison for one to three years or by confinement in the county jail for up to one year.

2. Theft in other cases is misdemeanor petty theft that is punishable by confinement in the county jail for up to six months, or by a fine of up to $1,000, or both.

SECTION 504 N.C.C. EMBEZZLEMENT

1. Every person who fraudulently appropriates to any use or purpose, not in the due and lawful execution of his or her trust, any property that that person possesses by virtue of trust, or secretes it with a fraudulent intent to appropriate it to such use or purpose, is guilty of embezzlement.

2. Every person guilty of embezzlement is punishable in the manner prescribed for theft or property of the value or kind embezzled.

SECTION 537C N.C.C. FRAUDULENT LOAN OF ANIMAL BY LIVERYMAN

1. Every owner, manager, proprietor, or other person, having the management, charge, or control of any livery stable, feed or boarding stable, who shall receive and take into his or her possession or control any horse, mare, or other animal belonging to any other person, to be kept and cared for, and who shall then knowingly and fraudulently loan the same, without the consent or permission of the owner thereof, is guilty of a misdemeanor.

2. A violation of this section is punishable by confinement in the county jail for up to 90 days, or by a fine of up to $500, or both.

SECTION 11357(B) N.C.C. POSSESSION OF MARIJUANA

1. Every person who possesses not more than 28.5 grams of marijuana, other than concentrated cannabis, is guilty of a misdemeanor.

2. A violation of this section is punishable by a fine of not more than $100.

SECTION 12031 N.C.C. DISCHARGE OF FIREARM IN PROHIBITED AREA

1. Every person who discharges a firearm in any public place or on any public street in a prohibited area of an incorporated city or an unincorporated territory is guilty of a misdemeanor.

2. A violation of this section is punishable by confinement in the county jail for up to six months, or by a fine of up to $1,000, or both.

SECTION 23152 N.C.C. MISDEMEANOR DRIVING UNDER THE INFLUENCE— ALCOHOL OR DRUGS

1. Any person who drives any vehicle under the influence of any alcoholic beverage or drug is guilty of a misdemeanor.

2. Driving under the influence of alcohol or drugs is a misdemeanor punishable by confinement in the county jail for a period of not more than six months and by a fine of not less than $400 nor more than $1,000.

SECTION 1320 NITA EMPLOYMENT CODE—DIVERSION OF EMPLOYMENT BENEFITS

1. Any person who is entrusted with money that is intended to be used in obtaining employment benefits and willfully fails to apply such money for such purpose and wrongfully diverts the funds to a use other than that for which the funds were received shall be guilty of a public offense.

2. If the amount diverted is more than $1,000, the person shall be guilty of a felony punishable by confinement in prison for one to three years, or by a fine of up to $10,000, or by confinement in the county jail for up to one year.

3. If the amount diverted is $1,000 or less, the person shall be guilty of a misdemeanor punishable by confinement in the county jail for up to six months, or by a fine of up to $1,000, or both.

JURY INSTRUCTIONS

PART I. PRELIMINARY INSTRUCTIONS GIVEN PRIOR TO EVIDENCE

01.01 INTRODUCTION

You have been selected as jurors and have taken an oath to well and truly try this case.

During the progress of the trial there will be periods of time when the court recesses. During those periods of time, you must not talk to any of the parties, their lawyers, or any of the witnesses.

If any attempt is made by anyone to talk to you concerning the matters here under consideration, you should immediately report that fact to the court.

You should keep an open mind. You should not form or express an opinion during the trial and should reach no conclusion in this case until you have heard all of the evidence, the arguments of counsel, and the final instructions as to the law that will be given to you by the court.

01.02 CONDUCT OF THE TRIAL

First, the attorneys will have an opportunity to make opening statements. These statements are not evidence and should be considered only as a preview of what the attorneys expect the evidence will be.

Following opening statements, witnesses will be called to testify. They will be placed under oath and questioned by the attorneys. Documents and other tangible exhibits may also be received as evidence. If an exhibit is given to you to examine, you should examine it carefully, individually, and without any comment.

It is counsel's right and duty to object when testimony or other evidence is being offered that he or she believes is not admissible.

When the court sustains an objection to a question, the jurors must disregard the question and the answer, if one has been given, and draw no inference from the question or answer or speculate as to what the witness would have said if permitted to answer. Jurors must also disregard evidence stricken from the record.

When the court sustains an objection to any evidence, the jurors must disregard that evidence. When the court overrules an objection to any evidence, the jurors must not give that evidence any more weight than if the objection had not been made.

When the evidence is completed, the attorneys will make final statements. These final statements are not evidence but are given to assist you in evaluating the evidence. The attorneys are also permitted to argue in an attempt to persuade you to a particular verdict. You may accept or reject those arguments as you see fit.

Finally, just before you retire to consider your verdict, I will give you further instructions on the law that applies to this case.

Part II. Final Instructions

1.00 Respective Duties of Judge and Jury

Ladies and Gentlemen of the Jury:

You have heard all the evidence and the arguments of the attorneys, and now it is my duty to instruct you on the law. You must arrive at your verdict by unanimous vote applying the law, as you are now instructed, to the facts as you find them to be.

The law applicable to this case is stated in these instructions, and it is your duty to follow all of them. You must not single out certain instructions and disregard others.

It is your duty to determine the facts and to determine them only from the evidence in this case. You are to apply the law to the facts and in this way decide the case. You must not be governed or influenced by sympathy or prejudice for or against any party in this case. Your verdict must be based on evidence and not upon speculation, guess, or conjecture.

From time to time the court has ruled on the admissibility of evidence. You must not concern yourselves with the reasons for these rulings. You should disregard questions and exhibits that were withdrawn or to which objections were sustained.

You should also disregard testimony and exhibits that the court has refused or stricken.

The evidence that you should consider consists only of the witnesses' testimony and the exhibits the court has received.

Any evidence that was received for a limited purpose should not be considered by you for any other purpose.

You should consider all the evidence in the light of your own observations and experiences in life.

Neither by these instructions nor by any ruling or remark that I have made do I mean to indicate any opinion as to the facts or as to what your verdict should be.

1.01 Credibility of Witnesses

You are the sole judges of the credibility of the witnesses and of the weight to be given to the testimony of each witness. In determining what credit is to be given any witness, you may take into account the witness's ability and opportunity to observe; the manner and appearance while testifying; any interest, bias, or prejudice the witness may have; the reasonableness of the testimony considered in the light of all the evidence; and any other factors that bear on the believability and weight of the witness's testimony.

1.02 Direct and Circumstantial Evidence

The law recognizes two kinds of evidence: direct and circumstantial. Direct evidence proves a fact directly; that is, the evidence by itself, if true, established the fact. Circumstantial evidence is the proof of facts or circumstances that give rise to a reasonable inference of other facts; that is, circumstantial evidence proves a fact indirectly in that it follows from other facts or circumstances according to common experience and observations in life. An eyewitness is a common example of direct evidence, while human footprints are circumstantial evidence that a person was present.

The law makes no distinction between direct and circumstantial evidence as to the degree or amount of proof required, and each should be considered according to whatever weight or value it may have. All of the evidence should be considered and evaluated by you in arriving at your verdict.

1.03 "WILLFULLY"—DEFINED

The word "willfully" when applied to the intent with which an act is done or omitted means with a purpose or willingness to commit the act or to make the omission in question. The word "willfully" does not require any intent to violate the law, or to injure another, or to acquire any advantage.

2.01 INFORMATION

The information in this case is the formal method of accusing the defendant of a crime and placing her on trial. It is not any evidence against the defendant and does not create any inference or guilt. The State has the burden of proving beyond a reasonable doubt every essential element of the crimes charged in the information.

2.02 PRESUMPTION OF INNOCENCE

The defendant is presumed to be innocent of the charges against her. This presumption remains with her throughout every stage of the trial and during your deliberations on the verdict. The presumption is not overcome until, from all the evidence in the case, you are convinced beyond a reasonable doubt that the defendant is guilty.

2.03 BURDEN OF PROOF

The State has the burden of proving the guilt of the defendant beyond a reasonable doubt, and this burden remains on the State throughout the case. The defendant is not required to prove her innocence.

2.04 REASONABLE DOUBT

Reasonable doubt means a doubt based upon reason and common sense that arises from a fair and rational consideration of all the evidence or lack of evidence in this case. It is a doubt that is not a vague, speculative, or imaginary doubt but such a doubt as would cause reasonable persons to hesitate to act in matters of importance to themselves.

2.05 BELIEVABILITY OF A WITNESS—CONVICTION OF A CRIMINAL OFFENSE

The fact that a witness has been convicted of a criminal offense, if such be a fact, may be considered by you only for the purpose of determining the believability of that witness. The fact of such a conviction does not necessarily destroy or impair a witness's believability. It is one of the circumstances that you may take into consideration in weighing the testimony of such a witness.

2.06 MOTIVE

Motive is not an element of the crimes charged and need not be shown. However, you may consider motive or lack of motive as a circumstance in this case. Presence of motive may tend to establish guilt.

Absence of motive may tend to establish innocence. You will therefore give its presence or absence, as the case may be, the weight to which you find it to be entitled.

2.07 DEFENDANT NOT TESTIFYING—NO INFERENCE OF GUILT MAY BE DRAWN

A defendant in a criminal trial has a constitutional right not to be compelled to testify. You must not draw any inference from the fact that a defendant does not testify. Further, you must neither discuss this matter nor permit it to enter into your deliberations in any way.

2.08 EXPERT TESTIMONY

A person is qualified to testify as an expert if [he] [she] has special knowledge, skill, experience, training, or education sufficient to qualify [him] [her] as an expert on the subject to which the testimony relates.

You are not bound to accept an expert opinion as conclusive but should give to it the weight to which you find it to be entitled. You may disregard any such opinion if you find it to be unreasonable.

3.00 CHARGES

The state of Nita has charged the defendant, Sarah Baker, with the crime of first-degree murder, which includes the crimes of second-degree murder, manslaughter, and criminally negligent homicide. If you are not satisfied beyond a reasonable doubt that the defendant is guilty of the crime charged, you may nevertheless convict the defendant of any lesser crime, if you are convinced beyond a reasonable doubt that the defendant is guilty of such lesser crime. The defendant has pleaded not guilty.

3.01 FIRST-DEGREE MURDER

Under the Criminal Code of the state of Nita a person commits the crime of first-degree murder if, after deliberation and with the intent to cause the death of a person other than himself, he or she causes the death of another person.

A person acts intentionally with respect to a result or to conduct described by a statute defining a crime when his or her conscious objective is to cause such result or to engage in such conduct.

Deliberation means that a decision to commit the act has been made after the exercise of reflection and judgment concerning the act.

To sustain the charge of first-degree murder the State must prove:

1. That the defendant performed the acts that caused the death of Kelly Baker, and

2. That the defendant acted after deliberation and with the intent to cause the death of Kelly Baker.

If you find from your consideration of all the evidence that each of these propositions has been proved beyond a reasonable doubt, then you should find the defendant guilty of first-degree murder.

If, on the other hand, you find from your consideration of all the evidence that any of these propositions has not been proved beyond a reasonable doubt, then you should find the defendant not guilty of first-degree murder.

3.02 SECOND-DEGREE MURDER

Under the Criminal Code of the state of Nita a person commits the crime of second-degree murder if:

1. He or she intentionally, but not after deliberation, causes the death of a person, or

2. With intent to cause serious injury to a person other than himself or herself, he or she causes the death of that person or of another person.

A person acts intentionally with respect to a result or to conduct described by a statute defining a crime when his or her conscious objective is to cause such result or to engage in such conduct.

To sustain the charge of second-degree murder, the State must prove the following propositions:

1. That the defendant performed the acts that caused the death of Kelly Baker, and

2. That the defendant intended to kill or cause serious bodily injury to Kelly Baker.

If you find from your consideration of all the evidence that each of these propositions has been proven beyond a reasonable doubt, then you should find the defendant guilty of second-degree murder.

If, on the other hand, you find from your consideration of all the evidence that any of these propositions has not been proved beyond a reasonable doubt, then you should find the defendant not guilty of second-degree murder.

3.03 VOLUNTARY MANSLAUGHTER

Under the Criminal Code of the state of Nita, a person commits the crime of voluntary manslaughter if:

1. He or she intentionally, but not after deliberation, causes the death of a person under circumstances where the act causing the death was performed upon a sudden heat of passion caused by a serious and highly provoking act of the intended victim, affecting the person killing sufficiently to excite an irresistible passion in a reasonable person. However, if between the provocation and the killing there is an interval sufficient for the voice of reason and humanity to be heard, the killing is murder.

To sustain the charge of voluntary manslaughter the State must prove that the defendant intentionally caused the death of Kelly Baker under circumstances where the act causing death was performed upon a sudden heat of passion caused by a serious and highly provoking act of the intended victim, Kelly Baker.

If you find from your consideration of all the evidence that this proposition has been proved beyond a reasonable doubt, then you should find the defendant guilty of voluntary manslaughter.

If, on the other hand, you find from your consideration of all the evidence that this proposition has not been proved beyond a reasonable doubt, then you should find the defendant not guilty of voluntary manslaughter.

3.04 CRIMINALLY NEGLIGENT HOMICIDE

Under the Criminal Code of the state of Nita a person commits the crime of criminally negligent homicide if:

1. By conduct amounting to criminal negligence he or she causes the death of a person; or

2. He or she intentionally causes the death of a person but believes in good faith that circumstances exist that would justify his or her conduct, but that belief that such circumstances exist is unreasonable.

Conduct means an act or omission and its accompanying state of mind or a series of acts or omissions.

A person acts with criminal negligence when, through a gross deviation from the standard of care that a reasonable person would exercise, he or she fails to perceive a substantial and unjustifiable risk that a result will occur or that a circumstance exists.

To sustain the charge of criminally negligent homicide the State must provide the following propositions:

1. That the defendant performed the acts that caused the death of Kelly Baker, and

2. That the defendant acted with criminal negligence, or she acted intentionally but believed in good faith that circumstances existed that would have justified the killing of Kelly Baker, and her belief that such circumstances existed was unreasonable.

If you find from your consideration of all the evidence that each of these propositions has been proved beyond a reasonable doubt, then you should find the defendant guilty of criminally negligent homicide.

If, on the other hand, you find from your consideration of all the evidence that either of these propositions has not been proved beyond a reasonable doubt, then you should find the defendant not guilty of criminally negligent homicide.

3.10 SELF-DEFENSE

The killing of another person in self-defense is justifiable and not unlawful when the person who does the killing actually and reasonably believes:

1. That there is imminent danger that the other person will either kill her or cause her great bodily harm, and

2. That it was necessary under the circumstances for her to use in self-defense such force or means as might cause the death of the other person for the purpose of avoiding death or great bodily injury to herself.

A bare fear of death or great bodily injury is not sufficient to justify a homicide. To justify taking the life of another in self-defense, the circumstances must be such as to excite the fears of a reasonable person placed in a similar position, and the party killing must act under the influence of such fears alone. The danger must be apparent, present, immediate, and instantly dealt with or so must appear at the time to the slayer as a reasonable person, and the killing must be done under a well-founded belief that it is necessary to save one's self from death or great bodily harm.

The State has the burden to prove that the killing was not in lawful self-defense. If you have a reasonable doubt that such was unlawful, then you must find the defendant not guilty.

4.01 JURY MUST NOT CONSIDER PENALTY

In your deliberations do not discuss or consider the subject of penalty or punishment. That subject must not in any way affect your verdict.

4.02 CONCLUDING INSTRUCTION

You shall now retire and select one of your number to act as presiding juror. He or she will preside over your deliberations. In order to reach a verdict all jurors must agree to the decision. As soon as all of you have agreed upon a verdict, so that each may state truthfully that the verdict expresses his or her vote, have it dated and signed by your presiding juror and return with it to the courtroom.

IN THE DISTRICT COURT
OF THE STATE OF NITA
COUNTY OF DARROW

THE STATE OF NITA	)	
	)	Case No. CR 2201–12
vs.	)	JURY VERDICT
	)	
SARAH HANNA BAKER,	)	
Defendant.	)	
	)	

We, the jury, return the following verdict, and each of us concurs in this verdict:

[Choose the appropriate verdict]

I. NOT GUILTY

We, the Jury, find the Defendant, Sarah H. Baker, **NOT GUILTY**.

Presiding Juror

II. GUILTY

We, the Jury, find the Defendant, Sarah H. Baker, **GUILTY** of the crime of:

Murder in the First Degree

Murder in the Second Degree

Voluntary Manslaughter

Criminally Negligent Homicide

Presiding Juror